D1245735

BEAUTIFUL SABRE

©2017 Edward K. Mills II

Published by Hellgate Press

(An imprint of L&R Publishing, LLC)

Hellgate Press
PO Box 3531
Ashland, OR 97520
email: info@hellgatepress.com

Cover & Interior Design: L. Redding

Cataloging In Publication Data is available from the publisher upon request.
ISBN: 978-1-55571-866-4

Printed and bound in the United States of America
First edition 10 9 8 7 6 5 4 3 2 1

Contents

BEAUTIFUL SABRE

A USAF Pilot's Memoir of Gunnery School and Flying the Storied F-86F

EDWARD K. MILLS II

HELLGATE PRESS   ASHLAND, OREGON

Dedication

THIS BOOK IS DEDICATED TO MY Princeton University roommates, Tony Ross and George Hackl. Both were United States Air Force fighter pilots.

Tony was in USAF flight school class 57-O. After earning his wings, he was assigned to Perrin AFB in Sherman, Texas for advanced interceptor training. From there he was assigned to an active duty squadron, the 49th Fighter Interceptor Squadron, Air Defense Command. The 49th was based at Laurence G. Hanscom Field in Bedford, Massachusetts. The aircraft Tony flew for the 49th was the F-86L. He returned to Princeton to attend grad school in architecture in November 1958.

Tony is a precisionist. My guess is that he was one of the finest jocks of the 49th, if not the finest.

George was in USAF flight school class 57-M. After earning his wings, he was assigned to Luke AFB in Glendale, Arizona, for advanced. From there he was assigned to an active duty squadron, the 310th Fighter Bomber Squadron, 58th Fighter Bomber Wing, Pacific Air Forces (PACAF). The 310th was based at Osan Air Base, K-55, in Osan, Korea. The aircraft George flew for the 310th was the F-86F. George returned to civilian life in June 1958.

Not long ago, George sent me the following note: "My overriding memory of the Sabre was that it felt like it was part of you and you were part of it. Like those thin leather gloves that we wore, you didn't even know you had them on. Whatever you thought of doing in the sky, all that complexity of machinery that surrounded you was thinking of exactly the same thing at the same moment. It was never ahead of you but there wasn't the slightest fraction of delay in its response. And it was nimble, smooth, fast, friendly. You could pull it around hard and it jumped with you."

Although George came to fly the F-86F for many more hours than I, we loved the bird in equal measure.

Prologue

HE ROAR OF A JET ENGINE BROUGHT US out of the dining room, onto to an aft deck. The ship was the RMS *Saxonia,* a Cunard Line passenger vessel sailing from Liverpool to Montreal. It was midday on an August day in 1955. My wife and I, newly married babes of twenty-one, were coming home from our honeymoon. Since June we had been traveling in France and the British Isles. Now the *Saxonia* was taking us west on the St. Lawrence River, headed for Montreal. From there we would go by train to New Jersey, where we would move in temporarily with my parents. There I would wait for orders from the United States Air Force.

We could see the airplane in the distance. The roar we had heard had coincided with its zooming up, over the ship. It then had turned away from the *Saxonia,* sliding behind, curving down to pick up the course of the river. Now it was skimming flat, just above the rippling surface, headed once again for the ship, about to make another pass. In an instant, it was beside us, level with the deck on which we were standing. It was so close it seemed we could touch it if we were to reach out. We looked into the face of the pilot, peering over at us through his gleaming,

Plexiglas canopy. The airplane was beautiful. It was a creature of fine design, wings swept back, made for speed, graceful and robust at the same time. And it flaunted a gorgeous, radiant color—cerulean blue. Later we marveled that someone in the Royal Canadian Air Force had been allowed, perhaps even authorized, to select such a color. Perhaps the pilot was a very important person? Or did the airplane itself, being beautiful, simply demand dazzling paint?

Now it was past us, behind us and above us. The noise was deafening. As we turned to watch, it rolled onto its back, climbing upside down. Then it returned to right side up, leveled off, arced right and sped away. It was gone. I said to my wife, "I think that beautiful airplane was an F-86. I believe it's called Sabre. Next year I might see more of them."

My schedule for the three following years was already known. In September I would join Exxon, taking a management beginner's job at their oil refinery in New Jersey. Then, perhaps before the end of the year, I could expect active duty orders from the Air Force. On graduation from Princeton University in June, I had been commissioned a second lieutenant in the Air Force Reserve, having completed four years of reserve officer training. In return for the commission, I had committed to three years of service. My hope was to be accepted into flying school and, in time, to learn to fly fighter planes. But that day on the *Saxonia's* deck it was beyond imagining that the fighter I would eventually fly would be the very same, beautiful Sabre.

One

Princeton

O NE SATURDAY AFTERNOON IN THE summer of 1951, not long
before I was scheduled to enter Princeton University as a
freshman, my father said to me, "We need to talk." It was an
unusual moment. He and I did not know each other very well.
When I was a little kid, he had been away in World War II. He
was commanding officer of a United States Navy ship of war.
Overseas. After the war, when he was home again, I was away
at boarding school. We did overlap, however, in the summers.
But even then we seldom saw each other. He was preoccupied at
work. He was striving, hoping to ascend to the presidency of a
bank in New York City (eventually he did). I also was busy. In
my teen years I always had summer jobs.

So I was apprehensive. He led me into the room in our house
that he used as an office. He sat behind a desk. I took a chair in
front. The afternoon sun streamed into the room. He got right to
the point. "I commend you for applying to Princeton University
and for getting in. Now we need to talk about how you intend to
discharge your military obligation."

I had no idea what he was talking about. About a year earlier,
the North Koreans had invaded South Korea and there was

fighting going on. However, word of it had barely penetrated the cocoon of my boarding school. I was vaguely aware that Americans were engaged in the conflict. Obviously they served in the military. Perhaps this was what he had in mind. So I said, "Do you mean Korea, sir?"

"Well, yes, to an extent. But my feeling is that people of privilege, like us, have an obligation to serve our country, no matter what the global circumstance, whether we—Americans—are at war or in peace. And I believe the best way for us to do that is to serve in the military. Voluntarily. More than that, I feel we should make every effort to serve as officers. We need, if we can, to help lead the parade."

Again, what he was saying was over my head. Although I well knew that he had been an officer in the Navy, I did not know how he became one and I could not even guess how I might become one. Or how becoming one would connect to my attending Princeton. I respectfully asked him to explain.

He told me that there were two paths I might follow. One was to sign up, on arrival at Princeton, to enter an ROTC unit. ROTC stood for Reserve Officer Training Corps. He explained that, at many colleges, including Princeton, ROTC units represented each of the three branches of the United States military: Army, Navy and Air Force. Boys who joined one of those units would, on graduation, be awarded commissions as officers in return for taking ROTC courses each academic year and attending military camp in the summer between their junior and senior year. The other path described by my father involved joining one of the military branches not as an officer but as an enlisted man. That could be done after graduation. Once introductory, enlisted training was complete, it would be possible to apply for admission to Officer Candidate School (OCS). Successful completion of OCS training would lead to an officer's commission.

After explaining all this, my father said, "Please make sure you understand. I am happy to pay for you to attend Princeton. But I am not going to do that unless you commit, before you enter the University, to follow one of the paths toward serving as an officer that I have described."

It occurred to me, in that talk with my father, that I was encountering something consequential. Before he had gone off to war, about a decade earlier, he had been a little older than I was as we sat together that summer day. But not much older. Probably he had been as blasé about the conflict that was then unfolding in the world around him as I was about the military training that he was describing now. Perhaps the idea of obligation to country meant as little to him then as it did to me now. But he had gone to war. He had spent a couple of years at war. Much in his life must have changed. Certainly he had changed. So now the subject he was discussing with me was, for him, deadly serious. It meant a lot to him. Furthermore, my grasping the importance of it was so important to him that he was willing to cast me out if I failed to comprehend it.

I got the message. I didn't hesitate. I thought the sooner I gave evidence of commitment the better. I told him I would sign up for ROTC as soon as I got to Princeton.

****

I had two uncles who had served as military pilots in World War II. As young men in civilian life before the war, both had owned small planes. My father's brother had kept his plane at an airfield in New Jersey. The day after the Japanese bombed Pearl Harbor, on December 7, 1941, he submitted an application to join the Army Air Corps as a pilot. Many young men had done the same thing. He was told to wait. Wanting to help, he had joined the Civil Air Patrol to fly hour after hour in daylight hours over the Atlantic, looking for German submarines. They were sinking American ships within sight of the Jersey shore. One sunny morning he had taken me to see his little airplane. He was getting it ready to go searching. I asked him if he had ever found a submarine. "Not yet," he said. "The ocean is a big place."

He never did find a submarine. They stayed submerged, hidden, during the day. A few months after he had shown me around, his application to join the Army Air Corps was accepted. For the rest of the war he flew transport planes for the Army. He flew throughout the United States and widely overseas. On a trip to Texas he had met a beautiful woman who worked as a stewardess for Pan American Airways. She had grown up in a little farm town called Pharr, Texas, in the Rio Grande Valley. They were married and, when the war ended, he brought her home to New Jersey. Years later in the family it was said that she never was truly happy away from Pharr. In 1956, her mother would come to call on my wife and me when we lived in the Rio Grande Valley town of McAllen. At the time I was attending primary flight school near there. But that part of the story needs to wait.

My mother's brother was the other uncle pilot. Before the war, he and a wealthy friend—each owning airplanes for pleasure— had set up a little airline. Their plan was to fly passengers and small freight from Wilmington, Delaware to Pittsburgh, Pennsylvania and back. Ahead of its time, the venture did not succeed. As a result, it appeared the uncle's flying days would be curtailed, if not ended altogether. But, not long after their airline failed, the Japanese attack occurred and the uncle immediately offered his services to the Army Air Corps. He also was told to wait. But soon enough he was called up. In time, he was assigned to the China Burma India (CBI) theatre. There he flew combat, shooting at the Japanese and being shot at in return.

Before being sent to the CBI, he was in charge of a training squadron stationed at an Army airfield near Washington, D.C. At that time, my mother, with her husband the naval officer serving overseas, accompanied by my brother, sister and me, lived with her parents at their hilltop farm in northern Virginia. Every couple of weeks, her brother the pilot would commandeer an Army airplane at his Washington station and fly the short distance south. He would buzz the hilltop. Sometimes he would appear overhead in the famous, twin engine Douglas DC 3. "C-47" was its formal, military name; the C stood for "cargo." The airplane was also called the Gooney Bird. Usually C-47s had at least two in crew, pilot and copilot, and sometimes there was a third man. He was a military mechanic, called crew chief. Free spirit that he was, the uncle wasn't shy about bringing the full crew with him when he came down to buzz us. He was casual about his flying, also. I remember one day seeing the passenger door of his Gooney Bird standing open as he banked around the farm house.

On other occasions he would buzz the hilltop in single-engine fighter planes, frequently the well-known, big, radial engine Thunderbolt. Its military designation was P-47; the P stood for "pursuit." Later, P would be changed to F, which stood for "fighter."

The Thunderbolts that the uncle flew were always painted green, ready to fight. As he turned low over our heads, he would have the airplane's canopy open so we could see his big smile. Once he buzzed us in the equally famous Mustang, the P-51. It was silver, perhaps fresh from the factory. It was more graceful than the Thunderbolt. Every time he came to see us we all—grandfather, grandmother, mother, brother and sister and I—would rush out into the field behind the house and wave.

So, when I arrived at Princeton and was thinking ROTC, the unit I wanted to join was the one that had to do with airplanes. It was the United States Air Force (USAF) unit. The name was no

longer Army Air Corps. During the war it had changed to Army
Air Force. After the war, the fliers had separated altogether from
the rest of the Army and had become the United States Air Force,
independent and free standing. As it happened, the Air Force
ROTC unit that I found at Princeton in the fall of 1951 was, like
me, brand new. The Air Force and I were arriving together.

It seemed the brass of the Air Force were determined, as new
kids on the block, to make a big impression at Princeton. The idea
was to at least match the appeal of the other ROTC units, the Navy
and the Army. I don't remember the history of the Navy unit. But
I do remember that the Army unit was well established and well
regarded. It had been on campus since 1919. It had a reputation for
turning out competent artillery officers. Army ROTC boys were
proud to go off to summer camp at Fort Sill in Oklahoma to learn
to fire big guns. The Air Force had to go some to match the Army's
standing. One of their first moves was to put a full colonel in charge
of the new unit. The insignia full colonels wear is a silver eagle,
clutching arrows. Accordingly, the nickname for full colonel was
bird colonel, or bird. Everyone in the military game knew that only
generals were bigger than birds. Army ROTC at Princeton had
never had a general in command. So the boss of the Air Force
ROTC unit immediately either outranked or at least equaled in rank
the Army's senior man.

And what a fine specimen that Air Force bird colonel was. I
remember him as being 6'2"inches tall or perhaps 6'3". He was
blond. He stood very straight. He had a barrel chest. He was a
fighter pilot. His eyes seemed to sweep the horizon. In the war,
he had served in the same CBI as my mother's brother. In that
theatre he had flown the famous Mustang. He had shot down
Japanese airplanes. His uniforms were handsome, especially the
summer one. It was striking in color, light tan with a silver cast.
Of course he wore not only his birds on his shoulders but, on his

left breast, silver pilot's wings. They rested atop a grand patch of many colored ribbons. And those wings weren't just ordinary, pilot wings, the ones I would earn five years later. Where my wings consisted only of a shield in the center with wings extending to left and right, the wings the colonel wore had a star on top of the shield and the star was surround by a wreath. The extra decoration signified that the colonel had accumulated lots of flying hours, perhaps as many as 3,000. Earlier, when he had collected something like 2,000 hours, his shield would have been surmounted with the star alone.

Working for the colonel were three majors. Two also were pilots, but not fighter pilots. I think their shields may have had stars on them. They had done plenty of flying, although not as much as the colonel. In the war they had piloted Gooney Birds, carrying paratroopers and cargo. They chomped cigars. They did the dirty work of the colonel's unit, teaching the dishwater dull subject called military science. They hated it. But they knew their pensions depended on their sticking it out, collecting the additional years of service needed to get them to the target twenty, when they could retire with an Air Force paycheck. The third major wasn't a pilot. He was a navigator. His wings were different. Their center piece was a globe instead of a shield, appropriately. I think there might have been a star on top and he too wore lots of ribbons.

Unlike the other two majors, he seemed to enjoy teaching. Because he occasionally managed to make military science interesting and had a sense of humor about being stuck with school boys, we liked him and the feeling was mutual. Happily for all three majors, a portion of the ROTC curriculum they were obliged to teach was quite painless for them and a treat for us. It consisted of gun camera films from World War II. The majors' job was simply to get the movie projector going. We were delighted. What we saw was Thunderbolts and Mustangs shooting at things. Sometimes their targets were other fighters, occasionally with men clambering out of cockpits as their airplanes were shredded around them. Sometimes they shot at structures called flak towers, which frequently shot back. Our favorite targets were trains. Frequently the shooters would hit engines and make them explode. Then whooshing up out of their smokestacks would come columns of white smoke, rising faster and faster. We would cheer.

Supporting the colonel and his majors were enlisted men. One was a cheerful sergeant who managed, on our graduation day, to be the first person to salute me as an officer. That morning I had just sworn to uphold (or was it defend?) the Constitution of the United States. I was striding off to find my girlfriend when the sergeant suddenly appeared, with a big smile on his face, announcing that he would "pop me a big one." Of course I returned his flamboyant salute and, answering his smile with a big one of my own, handed him a five dollar bill. That was the ancient military custom. Brand new officers gave money to the first enlisted man who saluted them.

There also was a master sergeant assigned to the unit. His rank was the highest enlisted rank at that time. He was a big, normally quiet man. He had enlisted in the Army before the war and transferred to the Air Force later. Occasionally he would brief us on some technical subject. I think it was he who told us about the 1911 model Colt 45 pistol.

In the course of one such briefing session, something one of us asked apparently reminded him of a ghastly time in his military life. He had been brutalized by the Japanese in the Bataan Death March. Suddenly, standing in front of us, in the middle of his talk, the big man was weeping. Then he was shaking, and cursing "those dirty little yellow bastards." We did not know what to do. Fortunately, one of the majors showed up. He comforted the distraught big man. Then led him away.

****

Soon after joining the Air Force ROTC unit at the start of my freshman year, I was issued a uniform. It was the winter model. Air Force blue. Its centerpiece was a formal blouse, or jacket, that extended down to the hip and was closed up the front with silver buttons. Underneath was a light blue shirt and blue necktie. Blue trousers, brightly polished black shoes and a dress hat with a leather bill and silver insignia front and center completed the regalia. I do not remember what insignia we, as officer candidates, wore. Officers and enlisted men had different insignia and I suppose ours was yet a third style. Soon after every candidate had received his uniform, we were told to assemble. This was to be the first time the brand new Air Force ROTC unit would come together. We were to meet on one of the beautiful Princeton playing fields. They were absolutely flat, carefully tended, lush green. One was to be our first parade ground.

When I arrived there, I was surprised at what I saw. First, there were boys in Army uniforms shouting. One of them strode up to me and yelled something like, "Form in that rank, candidate." Second, there were dozens and dozens of boys in Air Force blue. And more were arriving every minute. As the Army boys herded those of us who wore blue into ranks, the size of our contingent was startling. There were at least two hundred Air Force ROTC boys on the field. Because the freshman class in total numbered only eight hundred, this meant fully one quarter of them had chosen to join the Air Force ROTC. Did they all have fathers, or uncles, like mine?

Over time, I would learn that more than a few had fathers like mine. My Princeton roommate's father, for example, had been even more adamant than mine. Where my male parent had been relaxed enough to wait until summer to ask me what I intended, his father had challenged him on the day he graduated high school. Informed by the flustered boy that obligation to country didn't ring a bell, the father went immediately to outrage mode. He demanded that his son agree on the spot to join the United States Navy, doing so by joining the Princeton Naval ROTC unit as soon as he arrived at the University. In World War II the father had served for several years as an officer on the staff of Admiral Chester Nimitz, first at Pearl Harbor and later on the island of Guam, taken back from the Japanese. Cowed temporarily, the son assured his father he would join the Navy ROTC as soon as he arrived at Princeton. Three months later, when he got there, however, he regained a measure of self-respect and independence—joining not the Navy ROTC but, instead, the Air Force, determined to serve his country as a pilot. The father did not object.

Six years later the son spent two years in an Air Force Air Defense Command squadron as an active duty fighter pilot. His job was to protect the United States against foreign air attack. He flew a war plane every day. It was the F-86L, cousin of the beautiful Sabre. His father was proud.

The presence of the Army boys herding the boys in blue that afternoon on the Princeton parade ground was quickly understood. Because all the Air Force ROTC kids were freshmen, none knew how to drill or march or salute or do other, simple, military things. Because it would have been beneath the dignity of the colonel and his majors to chase us around a parade ground, and inappropriate for the enlisted men, the unit had borrowed older Army ROTC boys who had had some military training.

As to why there were so many kids in Air Force blue? One reason was indeed the influence of fathers, and uncles, like mine. Another reason had to be the widespread awareness at the time that the government was considering reinstating the draft that had been in place during World War II. So boys could conclude that it would be better to fly in Korea than to serve there in the infantry and, whether you could fly or not, it would be better to serve as an officer than as an enlisted man. Also, the colonel's men had done a good job of spreading the image of the Air Force around the Princeton campus. There were lots of posters of fighter planes, and horizon searching fighter pilots (some wearing G-suits, which I would learn about later) on display. They were to be found outside lecture halls and dining halls and on the way into the library and even at the entrance of famous Nassau Hall, where Madison and Wilson had sojourned.

Stepping into the rank as directed by the Army ROTC boy, I received shouted guidance. "Get that toothpick out of your mouth, candidate! And the next time I see you, candidate, you damn well better have that haircut. You look like a shaggy dog!"

Later in my Princeton days I came to know the fellow who shouted at me that first day. He was from a well-to-do coal mining family in West Virginia. Like me, he had been sent away to boarding school. His was a military school. So when he arrived at Princeton he already knew how to do military things. After he graduated, he served in the artillery and had a good record.

****

Just as the Army ROTC boys went off to Fort Sill, Oklahoma in the summer of their junior year, so we Air Force ROTC boys had a summer camp experience. In the summer of 1954, ours was at Greenville, South Carolina. The Air Force base there was Donaldson Air Force Base (AFB). The airplanes stationed at Donaldson were multi-engine craft. Some were newer versions of the venerable, twin engine Gooney Bird. Those were called Flying Boxcars. They had a strange look. The cockpit and cargo compartment was a sort of pod. It did not have the usual fuselage. Instead, it had two booms sticking out the back. Rudders to make the thing turn and elevators to make it go up and down were attached to the ends of the booms. We learned at Donaldson that sometimes the Flying Boxcars were called Flying Coffins.

The other airplanes that lived at Donaldson AFB were bigger, four engine creatures called Globemasters. They seemed huge, much larger than any airplane I had ever seen. They looked to be four stories high, or maybe even six. When they taxied around the airfield they moved slowly, their four engines humming. They were grand. Dignified. They were silver. We never knew exactly what they did for the Air Force. We supposed they transported people. But to what end? Both airplanes had numbers, of course. The Boxcars were C-119s. The Globemasters were C-124s.

Our summer camp activities were mainly drilling, exercising and playing games. At Princeton we had learned the rudiments of marching. I had been taught to call out, "To duh reahh, harch, by duh leff flank, harch, a bowut face" and so on. I even knew esoteric commands like, "Right ohh blee eek, harch." Every morning at Donaldson we spent two hours marching. It was hot. And the fields were not as flat as at Princeton and they were much dustier. Elderly Air Force captains supervised us. I must have made a favorable impression on some of them. Because frequently I was ordered to lead the formations of marching boys. I counted cadence ("Hup, hup, hup, leff rite leff") and gave commands and walked at the head of the parade. I have an ancient photograph of a formation that summer. I am in the front rank, calling out something. We all are clothed in jump suits of some sort. On our heads we are wearing pith helmets.

When the morning's marching was done, we would be ordered to change into T shirts and shorts for exercise. For an hour we would do pushups and jumping jacks and side straddle hops. Our contingent consisted of Princeton boys and an equal number of kids from Colgate University. We, haughty Ivy Leaguers, thought we

Plaque commemorating Donaldson Air Force Base, Greenville, South Carolina.

were superior. In marching and doing exercises, as best we could tell, we were. Our comeuppance came after lunch, when it was time to play softball. Naturally, we split up by school. The Colgate team turned out to be far superior. They had hitters who hit home runs. We did not. Also, from time to time they turned double plays. We never did. So we never won. As a final embarrassment, their players were not only more gifted athletically. They also were better looking.

When we finished summer camp, we could not escape the idea that we were one down to Colgate. They impressed us. We felt sure we would see them again, once we graduated college and our real Air Force days began. But we never did.

****

There were two other memorable moments that summer in South Carolina. One was a two part occasion that happened in downtown Greenville. Four of us Princeton boys were strolling on a Saturday, checking out stores. We came across a Ford dealership. In its showroom there was a car none of us had seen before. It was a gorgeous, first of its kind, Ford Thunderbird. Its lines were spectacular. It was painted bright yellow. One of the Princeton boys in our group was from a famous, Pittsburgh steel family. He had his checkbook with him that day. He bought the Thunderbird right off the showroom floor.

Later that same day we somehow learned that a girl was screwing all comers in a little apartment above a coffee shop on a Greenville side street. The Pittsburgh boy, flying high with his wonderful new car, went up to have a look. One of our softball players climbed the stairs with him. The girl told them how happy she was to see them. Her aunt, who was keeping her company, explained that she was just getting started in the business. A little while later the two boys descended the stairs, wearing big smiles. The third Princetonian and I were waiting for them at the bottom. We had been too timid to join in their escapade.

A year later, traveling in England, the Pittsburgh Princeton boy was introduced to an RAF fighter pilot who had fought in the Battle of Britain. The RAF fellow took a white scarf from around his neck, a scarf he said he had worn while flying in combat, and gave it to our classmate for good luck. When he arrived at USAF flight school (in his yellow Thunderbird) in the spring of 1956, he was wearing the scarf. Cleverly, he thought, he had that winter taken private flying lessons to prepare himself. So he was cocky when he started. The foot he got off on was the wrong foot. Neither the scarf nor his private flying lessons could save him. He washed out by summer. Washed out was the Air Force way of saying dismissed, dream of flying dead and gone.

The other memorable moment came and went quickly. One afternoon after softball we were informed that we would go flying in a C-124 that evening. After supper, a group of us were marched to the flight line. There we were told to climb up onto the bed of a flatbed truck with seats along the sides. We were driven out onto a runway where one of the monster Globemasters waited, propellers turning quietly.

Once inside the big airplane, we were seated on what seemed to be a lower level. We couldn't see out. But after a while we could tell that the big airplane was speeding along the ground and then it was flying, very smoothly slanting upward. For about an hour we sat talking to each other, wondering what would happen next. Then an officer came down a set of stairs that ran up one wall of the space we were in. One at a time, we were invited to climb the stairs and enter a little room. It turned out to be the Globemaster's cockpit. Two pilots were seated in it. They looked like boys, not much older than us. Each of them held onto a steering wheel of some sort. In front of them were windows on top of banks of gauges. Clouds could be seen through the windows. As each of us approached, the pilot on the left motioned us over. He told us to put our hands on the wheel that he held, saying, "I want you to be real careful. You can bank it a little bit. But just to the right." Then he moved his hands a few inches away and said, "Go ahead. Real smooth."

I did what I was told, or at least thought I did, turning the wheel slightly to the right. To my surprise, the whole huge airplane quite noticeably tipped in that direction. The pilot immediately said,

"That's enough." My flying experience was over. At least for the time being.

****

In the year I graduated Princeton, 1955, the Air Force had too many newly commissioned ROTC officers in its manpower pipeline. The boys who had signed up in that big wave in 1951 would have been useful to the Air Force had they gone on active duty right then, or even if they had done so a year later, or even two years later. But their deal was that they were allowed to finish college first, and by 1955 the Korean fighting had come to a stop. An armistice had been signed. So the need for the 1951 entrants was diminished. The Air Force told us to wait. The summer and fall went by. Finally, in the spring of 1956, a summons was issued.

Two

Moore Field

EVERYONE WHO JOINS THE AIR FORCE goes first to Lackland Air Force base in San Antonio, Texas. A Princeton classmate and I drove there. It took us a couple of days to get to east Texas from New Jersey and then what seemed a long time to drive halfway across the state to San Antonio. We were in a hurry to get there. We both were eager to fly.

Accordingly, the big moment in our short stay at Lackland was the physical examination administered by Air Force technicians and doctors to everyone who passed through the place. Appropriately, it was called "the flight physical." If you passed it, you had taken the first step toward joining the grand fraternity of pilots. Great men inhabited that magic realm. In the Air Force's song, which we boys knew by heart, it is called "the wild blue yonder." In fact, "Up we go, into the wild blue yonder" is how the song begins. Quentin Roosevelt, Eddie Rickenbacker, Jimmy Doolittle, Dick Bong, my uncles and legions more were the fraternity.

If, on the other hand, you didn't pass the flight physical, you would spend your Air Force years—as ROTC officers, we were committed to three years—in what seemed, in prospect, to be a sort of purgatory, doing the mundane work. Maintaining things. Supplying things. Watching radar screens at remote outposts. On the ground.

I was nervous about the flight physical. Because I have flat feet. The word was that you could be disqualified from Air Force flight school if your feet were flat. Somewhere I had heard that, in the course of the flight physical, which lasted several hours, the men being examined would unavoidably get their feet wet and the doctors would find evidence of flat feet in the footprints of the deficient. Thus forewarned, I spent every hour of the flight physical experience carefully, and unnaturally, walking on the outside edges of my feet, making, what appeared to me to be, non-flat footprints. The final event of the flight physical sequence was a meeting with a doctor. He was called a flight surgeon. As best I could tell, I had passed all the tests that I had been subjected to thus far. Vision tests, reflex tests, coordination tests. As I walked into his office in boxer shorts and T-shirt, the doctor (surgeon?) looked up at me and said, "Morning, Lieutenant." Then he said, "You have flat feet, don't you?"

Catastrophe. Purgatory. I said, "Oh shit, Doc." And then I received one of the many gifts that were to come my way, courtesy of the United States Air Force. Because the doctor next said, using language that was new to me at the time but which I immediately understood, "Don't sweat it, Lieutenant." Rejoice!

****

In June of 1955, ten days after I graduated Princeton and was awarded my officer's commission, my girlfriend and I were married. By the time Air Force orders directing me to Lackland arrived the following spring, she was well along in her first pregnancy. The considered obstetrical opinion of the day was that it would be best for her to fly out to San Antonio rather than make the long trip by car. She arrived, after a sunrise to sunset flight in a graceful, but slow, four-engine, propeller-driven airplane called a Lockheed Constellation, a couple of days after I had passed the flight physical. I knew I was headed for flight school, although I did not know where. Orders had not yet been written.

The first school I would attend was called Primary Flight School. It would be six months in duration. If a trainee managed to graduate primary, he would move on to a second school, called Basic Flight School. Completion took another six months. Success at Basic was crowned with the award of silver Air Force pilot wings. Wearing those wings, a boy would have joined the fraternity as the newest, fully-qualified-but-very-green member.

Eagerly awaiting orders, anxious to move on from Lackland, I showed my newly arrived bride a list of Air Force primary flight schools that I had managed to find. They were all in the South, where year 'round the weather is good for flying. From the list, we got an impression of the sort of places I would be assigned to next. The towns were all little ones. None of the names was known to us. Several were in Texas. Some were in Georgia, Mississippi and, I think, Oklahoma. One even happened to be not far from San Antonio. The town had the colorful Texas name Hondo. The following day was a Saturday, a day off for me at Lackland. I asked my wife if she would like to go look at the primary flight school at Hondo. Happily, she was as interested as I was. She suggested we go first thing the following morning.

Bright and early that day, off we went. On the outskirts of San Antonio we stopped at a gas station to buy an area map, then easily found our way to Hondo. It was a tiny, one street place. As we moseyed past the last store front, a gate with an Air Force sign of some sort materialized on our right. It was wide open. Because it was a weekend day, no one was there.

We drove in and proceeded cautiously, consumed with curiosity, along a narrow asphalt road between two rows of trees. Abruptly the trees gave way and we found ourselves on the edge of an airfield. Immediately in front of us, and to our right and left, as far as we could see, were airplanes. They were neatly parked, one after another. They were silver. They all were single-engine airplanes. There seemed to be two sizes, one about twice as big as the other. The bigger one looked a little bit like the Thunderbolt of my childhood. It had a big radial engine. Unlike the Thunderbolt, however, it stood up straight. I remembered having studied photographs of the Thunderbolt at rest on the ground, with its tail flat on the runway and its nose sticking up in the air. I had read that driving (taxiing) the Thunderbolt on the ground was difficult. It was necessary to turn the airplane from side to side as you went so you could see around the big nose. None of the airplanes we could see at Hondo would have that problem. All of them stood on three legs, their cockpits, fuselages and tails level with their noses, so their pilots would be able to see out the front as they taxied.

As soon as I arrived at my own primary flight school, I would learn that all the airplanes Air Force boys now trained in stood on the three legs we had seen at Hondo. Those legs were called tricycle landing gear, or tricycle gear. Fittingly, airplanes designed the way the Thunderbolt, the Mustang and most other fighters were designed in the old days were called tail draggers.

In my summer assignment to Donaldson AFB I had seen a full grown USAF facility. There were squadrons of airplanes, both C-119s and C-124s. There were pilots and other officers who had jobs on the ground and lots of enlisted men who worked for them and supported them. There were big hangars and numerous barracks and not a few office buildings. But none of those things had given me the sense of the United States Air Force that I got that quiet morning at Hondo. Even though all those silver airplanes were parked and, for the moment, still, it was clear what they were there for. They were to be used to teach boys to fly. When they weren't in that mode, they would be neatly parked, waiting to get back at it. Soon enough, they would return to work. That there were so many of them at Hondo itself made a point: the United States Air Force takes in lots of boys who hope to learn to fly. In those shining silver airplanes at Hondo, and in hundreds of other, identical airplanes at similar airfields across the United States south, the USAF would make many of them into pilots.

I realized that morning, in a way that I had not appreciated before, that I was about to become part of grand undertaking. Instructing hundreds, if not thousands, of boys to fly was a national enterprise, a considered expression of the will of the country. It was the United States of America that put all these airplanes in the Hondo woods and asked that they be used to teach boys to fly. How lucky I was to have an invitation to be one of the ones that would be taught. It was a second gift from the United States Air Force.

We didn't have long to wait before learning where I would go for primary flight training. The place was Moore Field in Mission, Texas. Mission is about 240 miles due south of San Antonio. It's in the Rio Grande Valley, at the very bottom of the United States. Like McAllen, Texas, its larger neighboring town to the east, Mission is located in Hidalgo County. It was best known for ruby red grapefruit. As my wife and I packed our station wagon for the drive south, we talked to neighbors about the Valley. We learned that rental housing is scarce in Mission. It was suggested that we try McAllen.

We first went to Moore Field to make known our arrival and find out when and where I was expected to report for duty. We were surprised to learn that Moore was not an Air Force base. Flying training was provided there by a private contractor. Day-

A commerative marker at the site of what was called Moore Field during World War II, then Moore Air Force Base during the Korean War. In the years immediately following the Korean War, when he trained there, the author remembers it again being called Moore Field. Today, it is no longer a military facility and is run by the U.S. Department of Agriculture as a private airport.

to-day instructor pilots, classroom teachers, bosses of both, mechanics who tended the airplanes and workmen who took care of the field were all civilians. Only the airplanes and a small complement of officers responsible for military matters were Air Force. I would soon learn that those officers, and therefore the contractor, did not call Moore's airplanes "airplanes." The Air Force word was "aircraft."

Departing San Antonio before sunrise, we sped south, leaving the King Ranch to the west and the great Hispanic American city of Corpus Christi to the east. We arrived Moore Field before midday. I was greeted, and promptly checked in, by a friendly civilian woman behind a desk in an office building. She told me to report, ready to fly, at 8:00 a.m. the following morning. She explained that my white, hard plastic, flying helmet, with earphones built in, and two, Air Force regulation flying suits would be issued to me then. She advised my wife and me to go to McAllen to look for a place to live.

As the two of us left the building, our attention was immediately drawn overhead. There was a great, buzzing aircraft noise. Aircraft were swarming. They were the same types of aircraft, big and small, that we had seen at Hondo. Some were slanting down to land. Others were turning in behind the ones that were descending. More were strung out behind them. In the far distance, against the bright blue, cloudless Texas sky, others could be seen gathering, getting into line to approach the field. What we were hearing and seeing, we would soon learn, was the conclusion of the morning's flying. The boys and their instructors in their aircraft were coming back to Moore for the midday meal.

In McAllen we found that most of the respectable rental places had been taken. Apparently numerous other Air Force boys and their wives had arrived ahead of us. Quickly we realized it would be best not to be picky. We ended up renting a one room apartment over a garage. The building was painted, strangely, purple. On one wall of the apartment was a Murphy bed. Air conditioning had only recently arrived in McAllen. Ceiling fans were standard. We considered ourselves lucky to have in our little apartment, in addition to a fan, one window unit. It was noisy and dripped. But it did blow cold air. As summer came on, we learned about south Texas heat. On some days, when the wind came up, we could see out our window that palm trees were bending. Remembering that breezes in New Jersey were almost always cool, we were taken aback at first to discover that the wind we stepped into as we left our apartment was hot.

Eventually we came to know that the town of McAllen had one public building equipped with central air. It was a hotel located in the center of town. It was called Casa De Palmas. It is still there. On weekends in the later days of our stay at Moore, we would take refuge at the Casa on ferociously hot days. It had a nice, air conditioned bar that opened onto a courtyard containing a pretty blue swimming pool. Several couples from the Princeton contingent at Moore—there were at least a dozen of us—would go there with our newborn babies, settle in the dark cool bar, drink beer and occasionally slip into the pool. The Casa was happy to have our business.

On the morning I reported to Moore Field at 8:00 a.m., I was issued my helmet and flight suits. Like coveralls, the flight suits zipped up the front and were liberally equipped with pockets, all of which zipped up too. I was informed that I was a member of Air Force flying class 57-M, sometimes called 57 Mike. That meant, if I graduated both Primary and Basic, I would get my wings in 1957. At Lackland I had learned that my Air Force serial number was A03050300. Symmetrical and easy to remember, I was happy with it.

Also appearing at Moore that morning were about a dozen other

Princeton boys and several dozen student officers from other college ROTC programs. We were all second lieutenants. The non-Princeton boys came from everywhere. Although we were the only Ivy Leaguers, there were graduates with us of other private institutions such as Southern California University, Southern Methodist University and Williams College. Land grant schools were also represented: Idaho, Nebraska, Oklahoma and Louisiana Tech. Just as we had mistakenly looked down our noses at the Colgate ball players at summer camp, so we Princetonians at first were discreetly scornful, in the Moore classrooms, of the boys who had not enjoyed what we were sure was our superior education. At least half of our time at Moore would be spent on academics. We were certain we could not help but do better.

Of course we were wrong. Smart boys came from all over the country. The best of them were equal to if not better than our best. We did discover, however, that their approach to academics was somewhat different than ours. Testing was frequent in Moore classrooms. As Princeton students we had been schooled in an honor system. On each Princeton test paper we were expected to write something like, "On my honor as a gentleman I swear that I have neither given nor received assistance in undertaking this examination." For us, the honor system carried over to Moore. To our naïve amazement, our non-Princeton primary flying school classmates, from the very first day, cheated. Notes were written on their hands and arms and shirts. Whispered sharing of information with neighbors occurred. Peeking at neighbors' test papers and inviting neighbors to reciprocate was common.

So the edge that some of those boys achieved in the classroom probably was unreal as well as ill gotten. But what kept us from discrediting the best of them, cheaters though they were in class, was how well they did in the aircraft. There they could not cheat. There their best was as good as ours.

I do not think of my academic experience at Moore as being worthy. I am embarrassed to recall, for example, that I was sufficiently uncaring in classwork that, if I ever learned what an all-important aircraft part called a solenoid was, I almost immediately forgot and, of course, have not the faintest idea today. Also, taking issue with the requirement that student pilots learn Morse code in the modern, highly technological world of 1956, when surely such a subject was no longer au courant, and thus learning it no longer necessary, I joined the non Princeton students and cheated on the Morse code test. I think I wrote on my sleeve. Illicitly I skated by.

****

On the first training morning at Moore, boys were introduced to their flying instructors. That took place in a building called a flight shack located on the airfield. It was next to what was identified as the flight line, where the aircraft were parked. There were several flight shacks at Moore. Each one held tables where instructors briefed and quizzed their students when they were on the ground. Each instructor at Moore had three students. So each table had four seats. My instructor was named Knox Faulkner. He was a man of about thirty. He had been a crop duster pilot. Somehow I knew that he had not flown in the military. But, obviously, he met USAF flight proficiency and technical knowledge standards. He was a smallish, well built, quiet man. Neither of his other students was a Princeton boy. I do not remember their names.

The two types of aircraft at Moore, as at Hondo and every other primary flight school, were the T-34 Mentor, the small one, and the T-28 Trojan, the larger one. T stood for "trainer." Both were fully acrobatic aircraft. The T-34 was made by Beechcraft. It had a Continental, in line engine producing somewhere over 200

A T-34 Mentor.

horsepower. It could fly, at most, 150 knots. One knot is slightly more than 1.15 miles per hour. I do not remember why the Air Force chose to express airspeed in knots. The T-34 was the trainer we would start in. If we succeeded in it, we would move up to the T-28. The T-28 was made by North American, which had built the Mustang. The T-28 had a Wright Cyclone radial engine offering about 800 horsepower. The engine was powerful enough to generate enough torque at full power, with the propeller spinning clockwise as seen from the cockpit, to cause the nose of the aircraft to want to turn in the opposite direction, to the left. It would do so with sufficient vigor during takeoff to require boy pilots (and all other pilots that matter) to stomp on the right rudder to keep the T-28 running straight, preventing it from veering off the runway to the left. I believe the T-28 could fly

The North American T-28 Trojan.

well over 200 knots. Perhaps, going downhill, it could reach 300. It was easy to fly and agile. It was a well-regarded bird.

Every boy's first flight at Moore, in the T-34, was called an orientation flight. When Knox Faulkner took me up, he flew around the Moore Field area, pointing out landmarks. He gave me a memorable little talk as we returned to the field and he opened the canopy in preparation to land. It went something like this: "This is the landing pattern. It's three legs of a rectangle. First is downwind, next is cross wind and last is final. Final takes you into the wind and down to land. We're now on downwind. Here you'll want to slow the aircraft down. As you get accustomed to flying the downwind leg, and the other two legs of the pattern, you will be able to tell how fast you are going without looking at the airspeed indicator. You will be able to tell by the sound of the air going by the cockpit." He was a good teacher.

The next morning I happened to run into a boy with whom I had attended boarding school. I had not seen him since he had gone to Williams College five years before. He had just completed primary flight training at Moore and was headed off to basic. I think he had been assigned to an airfield in Mississippi. He greeted me in a friendly way and asked how far along I was. I told him I had had my orientation flight the day before. He asked how it went. I told him that it seemed to go well, that I liked my instructor and that he seemed to have a friendly and positive approach. The Williams fellow burst out laughing. He said, "Just you wait. Tomorrow he'll start screaming at you. All the instructors here act nice and sweet and positive the first day. But they're all sons of bitches. You'll see."

Happily, Knox Faulkner never screamed at me. Perhaps he was one of the few instructors at Moore who wasn't a screaming son of a bitch? Or perhaps I caught on faster, or more skillfully, than my friend from Williams had and, as a result, Knox did not need to scream? I wouldn't ever know. But learning to fly from a man who did not scream was another gift from the Air Force.

If a boy managed to handle the starting days of Primary successfully, he was expected to solo after accumulating about ten hours in the air, guided in those hours by his instructor. The student pilot normally did not know just when he would be told to go up on his own. The usual sequence involved the student pilot and the instructor practicing touch and go landings together. As each touchdown was made, power was added and the aircraft took off again to be flown 'round for another practice landing.

On the solo day, the instructor would unexpectedly tell the student, in the middle of a touch-and-go sequence, to park the aircraft. He then would then exit the aircraft, saying to the student as he departed something like, "Lieutenant, you go ahead now and shoot a few touch and goes on your own." The instructor may also have told the student to finish up with a brief look around the area before coming back to land. When Knox Faulkner turned the aircraft over to me, I was a not too surprised. Other Princeton boys had already soloed.

Alone for the first time, I got the T-34 off the ground quite smoothly, shot the indicated touch-and-goes, briefly left the pattern for a little sightseeing and then, after about thirty minutes of solo flying, returned to the pattern, landed smoothly enough and taxied the aircraft back to Knox Faulkner with a nice feeling of accomplishment.

After I shut the aircraft down and climbed out, Knox and another student took over. I then went to the side of the runway to join several boys who were sitting there on a log, talking and gesticulating. The airfield we happened to be using was a called a secondary field. It was at a remote location some distance away from Moore. In that part of Texas, remote locations were all primitive. Rocky soil and scrub brush. I soon found out why the boys were gesticulating. They had found a family of horny toads and were feeding them crackers. Or trying to. For some reason at Lackland AFB I had heard quite a lot about horny toads. Maybe local boys were putting me on? Unexpectedly, the horny toads on the day I soloed were the only ones I ever saw.

As I drove home to McAllen from Moore Field that afternoon, thinking back on the horny toads and the solo flight that preceded them, I had a sinking feeling. Something about the "nice feeling of accomplishment" that I had experienced when I turned the T-34 back to Knox Faulkner and the other student now gave me heart burn. It seemed smug. It smelled of over confidence. My usual mode was different from over confident, if not the opposite of it. I was at least wary. There were kids at Moore Field who bragged and swaggered. I was leery of all of them. I thought at least some of them would come to a bad end. Already, some of the boys at Moore were having trouble; they were being held back from soloing. Even if they weren't struggling, would cocksure serve them well? Would they be bitten in the ass? I worried that the answer had to be yes.

My own comeuppance was not long in coming. On the day after my solo day I spent my time in the air with Knox Faulkner in the back seat. It was a normal training flight. It went well. The next day, I was sent off on my own. This would be my second solo flight. Having taken counsel of the worries experienced on the way home on solo afternoon, I felt I was neither smug nor cocksure. So I composedly departed Moore Field into the wild blue, planning to do the "look around the area" thing. All went well until the T-34 and I were climbing through 4,000 feet. Then I noticed a strange smell. Was something burning?

Looking around the cockpit, I saw something I had never seen before. The needle on the face of a control panel instrument immediately in front of me was persistently pointing at red. What the hell is that? That's the engine temperature gauge, dummy. It's telling you the engine is overheating. That's what's making the smell. Why on earth is the engine overheating? What could be making that happen? Oh for Christ's sake, it's the landing gear. You've come all the way up here without raising the gear! So the aircraft was pulling all that extra stuff through the air. No wonder the engine was hot.

I was so astonished at my own stupidity that I even hesitated to do what needed to be done, hung up momentarily on the idea that raising the gear at such an elevated altitude might somehow injure the aircraft. Oh for heaven's sake get on with it. So I yanked up the landing gear handle, watching with relief little green circles appear in each of the three little windows on the instrument panel that showed the positions of the wheels. Now they were where they should have been all along. I also saw the needle in the engine temperature gauge easing out of the red. I could only hope the burnt smell would be gone from the cockpit before we got back on the ground. And I would fervently hope that smug and cocksure, which seemed to have stayed around for another day, were now gone forever.

****

About half-way through the T-34 phase of my primary training, Knox Faulkner left Moore. I never knew why. He was replaced by a man who was as different physically as it was possible to be. He was huge. Perhaps 6′5″inches tall and close to 300 hundred pounds. It was a wonder he could fit in the rear cockpit of the T-34, where instructors rode. He had a typical Texas name—Bob Joe Carroll. In later years I came to know quite a few Texans with double first names. My favorite was named Bill Bob Draeger. What made Bill Bob special was that she was a woman— the wife of a senior fellow named Art Draeger for whom I worked at Exxon in Houston.

Bob Joe Carroll and I enjoyed flying together. Guiding me, he was gruff. But he never screamed. Our specialty together was doing acrobatics in the T-34. Because Bob Joe and I were a heavy load for the little bird, which didn't have much power anyway, some serious persuading of the aircraft was required. This was because acrobatics require airspeed and the T-34's Continental engine, even at full throttle, would only give so much. Accordingly, in order to get the additional knots needed for most acrobatic maneuvers, diving was necessary. Before we could dive, we first had to climb. So Bob Joe and I spent quite a lot of time coaxing our little bird up to altitude.

Our favorite acrobatic maneuver was the Cuban Eight. In order to do it successfully, we had to get the 34 to fly as fast as it would go. This meant flying downhill as much as possible. This in turn required our getting as high as possible to start with. Fifteen thousand feet of altitude is what we would try for. Arriving at that height, we would be ready to go. For us, hanging around up there wasn't a good idea. Because the air at that level is beginning to be short on oxygen. To spend more than a few minutes up there, your bird needs to be equipped with an oxygen system, as fighter aircraft are, or a pressurized cabin, as airliners are. Without such equipment, we would soon suffer from the shortage of oxygen, get a roaring head ache and, eventually, lose consciousness.

So, with the engine already at full power, with the altitude we wanted in hand, down we would go, gaining airspeed all the way. Once we had the needed knots of airspeed, we would pull the nose up and start climbing again, flying on our back as we rose. Then, with most of the height we had given up in return for more airspeed on the way down again regained, we would feel a stall coming on. The aircraft would have started to flutter as a way of warning that it would soon be unable to fly. Toward the top of our climb, it would be running out of lift, lift being the behavior of air in contact with its wings which enables an aircraft to fly. At that moment, realizing we could ascend no farther, we would level off upside down. Then, pulling the nose down, we would ease downward again. Inverted, we had come over the top of a vertical circle.

Then, still upside down, we would dive again. Soon we would roll over so we were again flying right side up as we descended. As before, after an extended dive, we would gain enough airspeed to once again climb. When, for the second time, we would arrive at the top upside down and then roll the aircraft upright, completing the maneuver. Looking at what we had done from the top of a nearby cloud, angels would have seen that we had with skill, with our little bird, traced a precise figure eight on its side.

In south Texas the land that was beneath us as we flew was primarily farm land. Unbeknownst to boys from New Jersey until they began to fly over Texas, most farm land in America (and perhaps in other countries as well?) is divided into parts called sections. Each section is one mile square, or 640 acres. From the air, sections march off to the horizon, from east to west and north to south. The boundaries of sections are called section lines. They usually are country roads. They are clearly visible and they too stretch on forever. When pilots in training learned acrobatics, they were taught to follow section lines. Maneuvers had to be done straight. Closely following section lines in the air above ensured that. When Bob Joe and I did our Cuban Eights, had the angels also looked down on us, they would have seen that both our dives and our climbs had all precisely tracked section lines. I never learned why the Eights were called Cuban.

One of the interesting, and unexpected, things that we immediately learned, as we began acrobatics, was where the earth and sky went when we rolled upside down or looped or did other, drastic maneuvers. I think when we started we expected that what we would see as we rolled, for example, would be the aircraft changing its attitude or orientation, switching from right side up to upside down with the earth staying where it was. Instead, what we discovered was that our view was fixed to the aircraft and, as a result, what changed in attitude, or orientation, was the world outside. In other words, as we rolled, the earth swung 'round us (pilot and aircraft), not the other way 'round. Similarly, if we were flying upside down at the top of a loop, as we rolled to return to right side up—thus performing the maneuver called Immelmann, named after a creative German flier in the First World War—it was the sky that relocated as we spun 'round, swinging back to its usual place above us. Another way of explaining this phenomenon is to imagine that the pilot and his aircraft are joined as a single being. When the pilot does acrobatics, he causes earth and sky to move around that being. Looking out, what the pilot sees is their movement.

****

As early as their ROTC days in college, boys who hoped to fly learned that not every student accepted into Air Force flying schools would graduate and get his pilot wings. It was generally understood that at least a third of each flying school class would be washed out. Some would discover that flying made them afraid. Their difficulty was officially called fear of flying. Some boys experienced it at first and then overcame it. Others could not shake it.

Another cause of washout was the inability to handle aircraft controls. For boys who happened to be left handed, this was to some extent unavoidable. The control stick which the pilot used to steer and maneuver the aircraft was positioned for the right hand. That stick projected up between the knees of the pilot from the floor of the cockpit. It activated the ailerons on the wings of the aircraft. Push the stick to the left and the aileron on the right wing would decline, giving that wing more lift, causing it to rise and leading the aircraft to turn to the left. Push it to the right and the reverse would happen. The stick also connected to the elevators at the tail of the aircraft. Push it forward and the elevator would depress, moving the tail up and the nose down. Pull the stick back, the elevator would angle up, causing the tail to drop and the nose to rise. If the right hand of a left handed boy wasn't dexterous, his ability to cause the aircraft to move the way he wanted it to move was impaired, making miserable his life as an aspiring pilot. Only the throttle, which controlled engine speed, was where the left hand tended to it. Not every leftie washed out. But some did.

Some boys, under pressure, could not remember even simple sequences. For example, the sequence of steps to be taken immediately following takeoff had four parts: gear clear flaps and power. It meant that the first thing to do after an aircraft left the ground was to retract the landing gear. The second was to clear the runway, moving over to fly beside it instead of immediately above it. The third, provided the aircraft had enough airspeed to fly without them, was to raise the wing flaps. The fourth was to reduce power from the 100% throttle setting used for takeoff to a lower, climbing speed, or cruising speed, setting. This sequence had to be learned and followed, every time.

Yet even a kid as diligent as I flagrantly failed to follow it. Amazingly, I had neglected the very first step. Having made that error as I brought the bird into the air, I even ignored it for minutes on end, remembering at last to raise the landing gear only after the aircraft itself at 4,000 feet as much as reached out and warned me, giving me both a pungent burnt smell and a plainly visible red needle. So it was not hard to imagine other boys making the same mistake, and perhaps making it more than once. Their doing so might well bring their primary flight school careers to an end.

Also, a few boys, whose misfortune it was to be assigned to an instructor who screamed, simply couldn't cope with that style of teaching. We all had heard of the student at another primary school who climbed out on the wing of a T-34, back on the ground after an especially abusive flying session, reached into the rear cockpit where his instructor was making notes on a pad, grabbed the pad and threw it away. He then hit the instructor in the face. He was gone the following day.

****

There was a process of guidance at Air Force flying schools, which for some student pilots was remedial and for others terminal. It was the awarding of pink slips. Probably the pad that was ripped away from the abusive instructor at that other primary flight school was a pad of pink slips. Each flight with an instructor was considered a flying lesson, even those enjoyable Cuban Eights with Bob Joe. Students who were judged to have failed any such lesson suffered the worrisome experience of being issued a pink skip. I presume in their wording those small, colored recordings of trouble explained what the failure was. Sometimes, I believe, the pink slip itself announced that the offending boy was to be washed out. Where he was to be given another chance, I presume the slip documented the remedial action that was required. I say presume because I was fortunate never to have received one, or even seen one. But is there any doubt that I would have received one had there been an instructor in the back seat when I climbed to 4,000 feet with the landing gear still down? My escape was narrow. In any event, there was an unwritten but well known rule: if a boy received more than a certain number of pink slips, he was washed out.

For whatever reason, those of us who did not wash out were not exposed by the Air Force to the boys who did. Nor were we acquainted with the process that was involved. We never saw them leave Moore Field. The routine governing our arrival at Moore each morning required us to muster in a military formation at 8 AM and march off, either to a classroom or to a flight shack. A boy who washed out would simply not appear on a particular day. It would be his failure to muster that would tell us that he had washed out. His absence would mean that there would be an empty space in the rank in which he normally marched. Military procedure then had us step sideways to fill the space, necessarily shrinking the rank. As time went by, our formations got smaller.

The Air Force was well aware of the pressure flying school students were under and the tension all of us felt. The pressure is part of the teaching design. Handling tension is expected of pilots. At the same time, the Air Force recognized that there comes a point in the process of learning to fly where some encouragement is useful. In the fifth month of primary at Moore, with fully one third of the student pilots who had started there already gone, those of us who remained were called together one afternoon by the senior military officer. He made a short, but very encouraging, speech. He started by telling us, in so many words, that we could take heart. We had survived the hard part. He finished by saying, "You men have done well. If you keep at it, you are going to get out of here with flying colors. Basic training schools will be fortunate to get you."

Early the following morning, my wife delivered our first baby, a little girl. My wife's mother had come down to McAllen to help with the big event. So it was my mother-in-law and I who were called to the hospital at midnight. At around 2:00 a.m., we were handed the brand new tiny creature by my wife's obstetrician. Back in the Murphy bed soon thereafter, I did manage to get a couple of hours sleep before heading out to Moore. That morning my assignment was to take a T-28 by myself out to a secondary field and practice touch-and-go landings. I had transitioned from the T-34 to the T-28 the previous week.

Each secondary field has a simple control tower where an instructor is stationed to oversee operations in and out of the place. That morning, Bob Joe Carroll was the man in charge. I found my way to the field without difficulty and flew the pattern we usually followed to get onto the ground. As Knox Faulkner had explained weeks before, the last leg of that pattern, the one which brought the pilot and his aircraft down to the runway, was called final approach.

As I turned on to it, from the previous leg called downwind, I was struck by how pretty the Texas sky was that morning. It also occurred to me to thank my lucky stars that my wife had had such an easy, and successful, delivery just a few hours before. Then, at exactly the right moment I was sure, I retarded the throttle and extended flaps to ready the aircraft to touch down. When I did that I was somewhat surprised to hear a noise in the cockpit that sounded like a loud and rather harsh musical instrument. Concentrating on achieving perfect alignment of the aircraft with the runway, I decided I would tend to the racket later. I then saw out of the corner of my eye a bright red flare, making smoke and sliding down toward the right side of the runway. Strange. Why is someone shooting flares? Then I happened to look over at the control tower. As I watched, a door swung open and here came Bob Joe, galloping down the front stairs of the tower, waving frantically.

Holy shit, he's waving at me! Finally I awakened and, happily, did the right thing. I pushed the throttle forward to 100% power, pulled up the nose of the T-28, raised flaps and cancelled the idea of landing just then. Until I did those things, I was about to commit a terrible flying error. I was about to belly land the aircraft. I had forgotten to put the landing gear down and was on the way to landing without it, ruining the propeller as it slammed 'round and 'round into the ground, damaging the engine itself and doing who knows what other injuries to the aircraft and perhaps even to myself.

All this was horrifyingly evident to Bob Joe, causing him to fire the flare and come running out of the control tower in a desperate, last ditch effort to get my attention and to wave me off. As I flew safely down the runway and climbed away, I realized what that racket had been. To save boobs like me from their own foolishness, from time immemorial aircraft throttles have been connected to aircraft landing gear and to horn systems. If a pilot retards power without putting his landing gear down, a loud horn will blow in the cockpit—warning the pilot of his error. Of course it is called the warning horn. How could I have so blithely ignored the warning? Turning downwind to get set up again for a touch and go, which this time would be properly done, I blushed with embarrassment. Soon I pulled back the throttle, put the gear down, lowered the flaps and turned on final. Would a pink slip eventuate? Bob Joe knew about the baby. He spared me.

****

The parents of the beautiful woman from Texas who was married to my father's brother lived in a little farming town just east of McAllen, and also in Hidalgo County, called Pharr, Texas. One weekday morning, with me out at Moore Field, my wife received a surprise visit from the woman's mother. It was the baby's bath time. The visitor, a tiny person, deferential and sweet, wearing a scarf on her head and boots on her little feet, helped my wife dry the baby and they sat and talked. She told my wife that she and her husband did row crop farming at Pharr. She said theirs had been a hard life. They were so proud of their beautiful daughter, and happy that she had been able to get away from farm life and marry a good man. She mentioned that there were a few pecan trees on their farm. As a gift for the young couple from up north, she had baked a small pecan pie. She gave it to my wife, apologizing for its size, saying something about the year's crop of pecans. Although we had never heard of pecan pie, we came to think of it as a special delicacy. In future years it was a happy reminder of Texas and the Rio Grande Valley. We asked for it in restaurants as we traveled in America. Over a lifetime, from time to time we found it.

****

About half of the Princeton boys at Moore were married and, like me, had their wives with them. The others were either single or married with their wives living at home. Apparently the married boys whose wives were at home thought that primary flying school, with success, and thus duration, not guaranteed, was an experience best undertaken by bachelors.

There was a feature of temporary residence in the Rio Grande Valley that was especially appealing to all Princetonians, married, single and bachelor, and non Princetonians. It was proximity and easy access to Mexico. Across the Rio Grande from Hidalgo County was the thriving Mexican town of Reynosa. There was a restaurant in Reynosa called the Cucaracha that many of the Moore boys and their wives frequented. The mariachi music was festive and the food exotic. Another place in Reynosa that, as far as I know, only the single boys, and perhaps the bachelors, frequented, was called Boys Town. It was said to be a sprawling place with dozens if not hundreds of Mexican women and girls doing prostitution. Also offered in Boys Town were what were called in those days "blue" movies. Some Princetonians were said to visit Boys Town just to take in the films on offer. Showing off his Ivy League liberal arts education, one Princeton boy wrote and distributed to the rest of us weekly movie reviews. I remember one particular headline: "Don't miss this one. Girls do it with animals."

****

Toward the end of the T-28 phase of primary flight school at Moore, about a month ahead of graduation, we were advised that we would soon do flying at night. I don't remember any particular preparation. One day we were simply told to wait around after normal classroom and flying hours until dusk came. We then were directed to climb into T-28s and take off. Our assignment was simply to fly carefully around the area, watching out for the wing tip lights and the tail lights of other aircraft. After a specified amount of time, we were to return to the landing pattern and put the aircraft back on the ground. We did that, entirely without incident. Finding the runway was no problem as it was outlined with little white lights along each side. Because the lights told us well enough where the runway surface was, landing was virtually the same as it was during the day. A difference that we did notice was in the quality of the air. At night it was smooth. During the day, in contrast, it was almost always bumpy. With the sun shining, heat rises off the ground, usually in columns of air. Some of those columns are small, some are large. Passing through the large ones, the aircraft notices, occasionally heaved up and dropped down again abruptly. In the cool air at night that didn't happen.

Closer to graduation, we were instructed to combine night flying and navigation. Our task was to depart Moore at sunset, fly north for a while to find a little town—I think it was Falfurrias or perhaps Alice—and then go southwest for a while to the heart of Mission and then return to Moore. We were said to be navigating by dead reckoning. The word dead meant deduced, or planned. Using that approach, our assignment was to prepare in advance a plan for the trip we were to make, using a map, plotting compass headings and calculating time intervals required to fly from place to place at projected airspeed. Once in the air, with the map on his knee, the pilot follows the plan as best he can, making adjustments as he finds he is off course one way or another or late or early in arriving at designated way stations. Instructors gave half serious guidance: if you get lost, go find railroad tracks and follow them to a town. Then fly down low enough to find a railroad station then read the sign on it that tells you the name of the town. There was always a funny punch line. When you're following those railroad tracks, keep your eyes peeled for aircraft coming the other way. Because there's bound to be a Navy pilot doing the same thing you are doing. There were United States Navy flying schools in Corpus Christi and Beeville, Texas, not far down the road from Mission.

None of us took the night time navigation exercise too seriously. This was because we all knew, for reasons now unknown, that it would be scheduled on a Friday night. In Texas, Friday night was high school football night—as the rest of America would eventually learn. In Hidalgo County, when we were there, one of the biggest, if not the biggest, of football stadia was in Mission. So almost always there was a game in that stadium on Friday night. In 1956, Mission was a modest town. Ruby red grapefruit. But there was nothing modest about its stadium or the lighting system that provided illumination on Friday nights. From the air, the place could be seen for miles. It provided an extraordinary, huge, upside down pyramid of light. So our navigation was a cinch. At first, we flew north for a while, cruising along for the number of minutes required to cover the distance to the way station in that direction. We then reported by radio to Moore that we had arrived Falfurrias or Alice, no matter where we actually were. Next we turned left and flew southwest for a while, aiming in the general direct of the gleam on the horizon that we knew would appear. When it did, we knew where to steer. When we actually arrived over the Mission stadium, with our aircraft cockpits full of football game light, we reported in again and then turn left for home, knowing Moore was just a hop, skip and jump to the east. Landing at Moore in the cool air, with the navigation mission successfully accomplished, was a piece of cake.

****

When it actually came time to graduate, the consensus of the class of 57-M was that a stag party celebration should be organized. A committee was formed. In due course, it was decided that graduation called for nothing less than a blue movie. In keeping with the propriety of the occasion, it would be shown in a proper venue on the American side of the Rio Grande. The committee was resourceful. Somehow a film that featured the most renowned of blue movie stars of the day, Candy Barr, was found. Perhaps it came from Mexico. An American Legion hall was rented by the committee for the showing. On the big night, the place was jammed. The word had gotten around to classes other than 57-M. Plenty of student pilots who were weeks and even months away from graduation —undoubtedly including some wouldn't make it— crashed the party. In keeping with the mores of the time, Candy Barr, who looked like a nice blond school teacher, was shown as willing only to offer conventional sex. When a customer demanded oral service as well, Candy Barr refused. She did not do that! At the customer's insistence, Candy cheerfully enough telephoned someone and asked if a woman could be found who would oblige him. Also in keeping with the mores of sixty years ago, a brown skinned lady appeared. She looked a bit down on her luck. Perhaps for that reason, she was agreeable. The movie ended with everyone happy.

****

After Moore Field primary classroom work and primary flying ended, there was a little gap of time for class 57-M. Apparently Air Force basic flying training schools, where we were to go next, weren't quite ready for us. So we were on vacation, waiting to be told of our new destinations. It was autumn. The heat of summer had begun to ease. In Texas, hunting season had begun. Men, women and children hunted. Their quarry included all manner of wild game: white tail deer, mule deer, mountain sheep, mountain goats, coyotes, bobcats, javelina (feral pigs, of which there were thousands if not millions in the state), wild turkeys, all species of ducks, four types of geese (specs, blues, greater Canadas and lesser Canadas), mourning doves, white wing doves, quail, squirrels and muskrats were species Texas boys told us about.

Late one windy afternoon, one of those Texas boys—he had played quarterback at Southern Methodist—and I crouched in a hedgerow next to a farm pond, hiding from mourning doves zooming down over our heads. As was their days' end habit, the doves were descending toward the pond, hoping to drink before their bedtime. Doves fly very fast and they zip up and down, erratically. They are hard to hit. Accordingly, we hoped to shoot them as they slowed "on final approach," getting ready to land. The Texan owned several shotguns and had loaned me one. As a novice hunter, I shot many times. But I did not hit. To his chagrin, the Texan did not hit either.

We had hoped to bring doves to our wives to barbecue. Instead we went out for supper, dining on what was called Tex Mex food. Our choices that evening were dishes that only in later years would become known in the rest of America: guacamole, enchiladas, refried beans and rice and a dessert called *sopapillas*, a delicate, sugared pastry into which honey was poured. We drank Lone Star beer. We considered it the best of the several Texas beers. Jax and Pearl were two others that were well known then. They are gone now.

****

In anticipating our next Air Force station, we had a sense that two considerations would determine where we would go. First, each Primary graduate was asked to state a preference. Did he want to fly single-engine aircraft or multi-engine aircraft? Sometimes instructors, or their bosses, encouraged certain Primary flying school graduates to opt for multi-engine school. Those of us who wanted to fly single-engine aircraft—fighters we hoped—and were not discouraged from stating a preference for them, not so secretly thought that boys steered to multi-engine training were being told that they were second rate. However, I never got the idea that the multi-engine boys much cared. They were quite happy to be aimed for big birds that they would be able fly to and from anywhere in the world. The rest of us could have the little puddle jumpers.

The second consideration that we thought counted in determining where we would go next was our class standing at Moore Field. However, none of us knew what our standing was. Apparently the management at Moore Field didn't want us to know. Nor, for that matter, did we have any idea of which basic flight schools were thought to be better than others, not to mention why. We did know some numbers. For example, there were at least two multi-engine basic schools in Oklahoma and no fewer than three single-engine basic schools in Texas. The Oklahoma locations were Enid and Edmond. The Texas ones were Laredo, Big Spring and Del Rio. As far as we knew, they all offered the same basic flight training. Later, at gunnery school, I found myself wondering if the basic flight training I received was, in some respects, at least, superior to that offered elsewhere.

However, there was an event that occurred during our vacation that shed a little light on one of the three, single-engine locations.

One morning when 57-M was in middle of performing some final chore out at Moore, a jet aircraft buzzed the field, then circled around and landed. As far as the students knew, this was the first time a jet had come to Moore Field. Two Air Force first lieutenants climbed out of the aircraft and soon we all were invited to meet with them. They seemed like salty fellows. One was memorably named Lieutenant Malcolm Toof. He will appear again in this story. That morning he told us that he was stationed at Laughlin AFB, that it was located in Del Rio, Texas, that Del Rio was the lamb's wool capital of the world and that Laughlin AFB had the best basic training school instructor pilots in the whole USAF. He said that the aircraft he had arrived in was a T-33, commonly called a T-bird. It was the aircraft we would fly if we came to Laughlin. The T-bird was the two-seat version of the F-80, a single-seat fighter called Shooting Star. The F-80 was the Army Air Force's first jet fighter. Dick Bong, World War II ace of aces, died test flying one in 1945.

Lieutenant Toof urged us all to sign up for Laughlin AFB. He spoke fondly of fighters, mentioning in particular the P-47—he called it the jug—as if he had flown it at one time. Perhaps he had caught the end of World War II. He said we would enjoy flying the T-33. After an hour or so, he and his companion took their leave. Somewhat to our surprise, they taxied their aircraft well out into the grass beyond the end of our Moore Field runway. Apparently the T-33 required a considerably longer takeoff roll than our T-34s and T-28s. As Lieutenant Toof got airborne, it seemed he just barely squeezed up and over the palms that lined the far end of Moore Field. But then, after briefly disappearing toward the Rio Grande, he reappeared. He had his aircraft right down on top of those same palms, coming back the other way, low and fast, now dipping down, engine roaring, to just a few feet above our runway, all the way to the far end and then up and away, zooming off, to Del Rio! We cheered.

Although we never knew our class standing at Primary, we could assume that it had three elements. One probably was some sort of military appraisal, developed by the little cadre of Air Force officers stationed at Moore. Those officers in turn relied at least in part on evaluations of their fellows provided by student officers appointed as prefects, or officer assistants, early in the Moore Field primary flight school session. Perhaps these fellows had achieved some sort of elevated rank in their home ROTC units. The evaluations they developed pertained to athletic accomplishment and to military bearing, appearance and courtesy.

In the athletic category, which was based on calisthenics, sprints, agility and obstacle course drills, I had done well. My score was the first place score in 57-M at Moore. In the military category, in contrast, I may have finished in last place, my performance and behavior downgraded because I had picked a fight with an officer assistant. A football player from Louisiana Tech, he had severely bullied a large, but not very athletic, Princeton classmate of mine one Sunday afternoon at the Moore swimming pool. I had come upon the fracas as it was ending, too late to help the Princeton boy while he was under fire. Even as he departed the scene, I felt obliged to do something to redress the balance. I thought I could take the bully, even though he weighed at least fifty pounds more than I did. I was sure his weight advantage would be lost so long as we fought in the water. I was determined to try. So I jumped in and went for him.

Starting beneath the surface, I soon had him upside down, my left arm around his waist, hooked to my left leg, my right fist clutched tight in his hair, ducking his head, pushing him under then letting him up again. After a few minutes of this, I held his head beneath the surface for a long count, yelling at him that he might be smart to "holler uncle." Blubbering, he did. He surrendered. I let him up. Slinking off, looking back at me, he muttered, "You little son of a bitch." I offered him my best, steel-eyed stare. Would it have been logical to assume that he was giving thought to downgrading my Moore Field military evaluation?

The second consideration that we thought counted in determining where we would go next was our standing in the classroom. Each of us probably had a composite of text scores. I imagined mine was at least equal to the average.

The third, and perhaps most important determinant, was a flying grade. Probably it had two parts. One was a day-in, day-out assessment by the instructor, or instructors, who regularly taught the student. The other must have consisted of grades given by checkride instructors. Checkrides amounted to test flights where instructors other than a boy's own examined him in the air on various aspects of flying. Subject matter could include some or all of what he, as student, had been taught: taxi, takeoff, normal landing, emergency landing, climb to altitude, level off at altitude, level turns, climbing turns (called chandelles), figure eights in level flight, acrobatics, entering the landing pattern, radio calls and radio procedures, navigation, spins and spin recovery, trimming the aircraft, slips, skids, crosswind landing and so forth.

In recalling my own primary experience, I have discovered something unexpected. Of all the checkrides I must have taken, I remember only one. It was in the T-34. I remember it because I did not do well. Before the ride, Bob Joe had told me to make sure to maintain a constant airspeed as I climbed the aircraft to altitude. He said my doing that would be very favorably noticed by the checkride instructor.

At that moment in my flying career I may have been as dutiful a kid as there was, certainly as determined to do well as any and absolutely mindful of the importance of the guidance of Bob Joe, and Knox before him. So, as I brought the aircraft upward, my left, throttle hand was keeping power precisely fixed, my right, stick hand was holding the nose of the aircraft just where it should be and my gaze was glued to the airspeed indicator—all of this concentration intended to guarantee that the T-34's climbing airspeed was exactly what it should be and as constant as steel. Just the way Bob Joe said. As the T-34, carrying the checkride instructor and me, with what I hoped was precision, rose in the sky, I would sneak glances in the little bird's rear view mirror. I thought sure I would see the checkride instructor admiring our rock steady airspeed. To my surprise, he did not seem interested. As far as I could tell, he paid no attention to our airspeed. Instead he was persistently, and quite noticeably, looking out of the cockpit. Sometimes backward and down. Sometimes upward and ahead.

Finally, in a hard voice, and to my dismay, he said to me, "Lieutenant, don't you ever get your head out of the cockpit? Don't you understand that there are other aircraft out there? Do you think the way you are flying is smart? Or safe?"

My chagrin was great. Clearly I had done wrong. That hadn't happened before. Did I stammer something about our climb out airspeed? I do not remember. But I do recall, before the ride was over, making another faux pas that seemed, at first at least, to again greatly trouble the checkride instructor. It occurred about an hour after the regrettable, head in the cockpit moment, when it had come time to return to Moore Field and put the aircraft back on the ground.

During the hour in the air, I felt I had managed to perform reasonably well the maneuvers specified by the checkride instructor. I had carefully followed the required procedures. At least there had not been a new disaster, although I felt my touch on the controls had been shaky. Happily, the stressful session would soon come to an end. So I searched for, then spotted, another T-34 out in front of us which was obviously headed back to Moore. In proper fashion I took up adequate spacing behind him and then turned to assume the heading he was on. Again came that hard voice: "Were you planning to send 487 to the end of the line, Lieutenant Mills?"

Holy shit! There was tail number 487, wing up and turning away, only a few yards off to our left. Had I cut him off? I had never come anywhere close to making that kind of mistake before. After a foreboding, quiet moment, the checkride instructor added, "Well, maybe he fucked up too. So we'll talk about it when we get back on the ground. In the meantime, how 'bout giving me a damn good landing so we don't have to write off this trip altogether!"

Although my landing was smooth and precise, when we returned to the flight shack I was apprehensive. I knew I had performed badly. To my surprise, however, the discussion at the table was not too bad. I was told to be careful about getting my head stuck in the cockpit and to be sure to realize that there are always dummies screwing up in the pattern. To my great relief, the near miss as I entered the pattern was not thought to be my fault. There was neither a pink slip nor even a sign of one.

It occurs to me sixty years later that probably I don't remember other checkrides because none was a problem. I did well enough in all of them. So perhaps I was among the more successful graduates of primary flying school at Moore Field. Although my military ranking may have been in the tank, my classroom grades may even have been above average. Perhaps my flying grades also were above average. At the time, I was not confident of that. My most clear memory is of being a little afraid every day. Not afraid of flying. I liked the aircraft, and flying, a lot. I made mistakes but not too many. The big ones were either private, as in the instance of the landing gear not retracted in the T-34, or forgiven, as in the case of the landing gear not extended in the T-28 on my daughter's birthday. My fear stemmed from being eager to please, wanting to succeed and, at all costs, not to become overconfident. Perhaps all of that was fortunate. I would find that my experience at basic flight school would turn out well. What had gone before at Moore Field must have helped.

Our little autumn vacation at Moore lasted only a few days after the visit of Lieutenant Toof. It came to an end with an episode that reminded us that what we were doing wasn't care free. No one was killed nor anyone injured. But the incident transfixed Moore Field for a couple of hours while preparations were made for what could have been a destructive, and even deadly, accident.

A new instructor had come to Moore. He was a former Navy pilot who had flown on carriers. The word had gotten around that he was a likeable fellow. He was cheerful. He had a positive attitude and he

was said to love flying. Late one afternoon, he and a student pilot
from the flight training class that followed 57-M at Moore were
bringing at T-28 back to the field when the problem occurred. As
the aircraft turned onto final with its gear down, the mobile control
person whose job it was to scan through binoculars each approaching
bird noticed that the nose wheel was aligned at right angles to the T-
28's forward and back axis. The aircraft was advised to abort the
landing and go around again. It was suggested that the landing gear
be cycled—brought back up and then lowered again. It was thought
that this probably would solve the problem, with the up and down
motion influencing the nose wheel to get straight. It did not.

As it happened, the whole of 57-M was at Moore that afternoon,
even though our duties there were largely complete. Perhaps we
were turning things in, or getting last minute departure instructions.
As was usual in the military, we quickly heard the news of trouble.
Soon released from whatever it was that we had been assembled to
do, we all, superiors included, went out to the runway to watch. We
all knew that what we might get to see could surpass the very worst
of car wrecks.

About 1,000 feet over our heads, two T-28s were circling the
field. The one on the lead apparently was the one with the problem.
The bird tagging along, in what we would learn in later training was
called the "chase" position, was ostensibly providing assistance.
The Moore Field PA system was opened to the radio frequency that
the two instructors, the chase pilot and the former Navy pilot, were
using to talk to each other. So we could hear what was being said.
Although we found it hard to imagine how the second bird could
be of much help, the chase fellow repeatedly assured the Navy chap
that he was there in case he was needed. We guessed, with all
cynicism, that tagging along behind an aircraft in trouble, even
though uselessly, may have even been required by Air Force
tradition. Or at least it was important for the sake of Moore Field

appearances? It also occurred to us that the "crisis" gave the second instructor an opportunity to fly what looked to us novices like a sort of formation position on the Navy fellow. His radio chatter gave us the sense that he liked that.

The reason the two T-28s were stooging around up there soon became apparent. They were waiting for the fire trucks of Moore Field to play their role in the drama. It now was only those lumbering fellows whose ministrations might avert tragedy. Absent their good work, the sequence envisioned was potentially gruesome: the Navy pilot would land his T-28 on its main landing gear and hold the nose gear off the runway as long as possible. But eventually, inevitably, it would fall, bringing the sideways facing wheel into slamming, skidding, screaming contact with the concrete surface. The nose wheel strut then would snap off, the aircraft would tip over forward, its propeller coming into splintering contact with the runway, hurling fragments in all directions, possibly puncturing cockpit and fuel tanks, maiming men and starting ghastly fires.

Aiming to prevent all this, what the fire trucks were doing was laying down foam on the runway. The idea was that the Navy pilot would land in it on his main gear only. He would hold the nose gear off the runway as long as he could. When it would finally fall, it would drop into the foam. Either the sideways wheel would slide smoothly along on the foam slicked runway surface, still sideways but untroubled, or it would respond magically to the foam by swiveling to straight forward and straight back, returning to its proper position. Either way, the day would be saved.

In the jaundiced opinion of kibitzing 57-M, the fire trucks were overworking the problem. The foam blanket they laid stretched most of the length of the runway. We thought it was much more foam than the Navy pilot needed. He could put the aircraft down with far greater precision than the extended foaming implied. Some of us thought he would be insulted.

To fashion their elaborate masterwork, the firemen had spent more than an hour spraying, huffing and puffing, back and forth. As a result, the sun was largely down by the time we heard someone on the PA system instruct the Navy pilot to bring the T-28 down. He promptly complied, turning on landing lights, easing down final, touching down skillfully, as we knew he would, at the front end of the strip of foam, leaving yards and yards of the stuff unused and unneeded.

For a short distance he slid along on two wheels as specified, pushing the foam up in a little wave. Then the nose of the bird came down. In the semi darkness, we couldn't see what the nose wheel itself did. Did it slide along sideways or straighten itself out? No matter. The wheel didn't catch on the concrete, the nose gear didn't break, the prop didn't smash and a catastrophe didn't happen. The show was suddenly over.

Maintenance people in boots went out to the aircraft. The Navy fellow and his student climbed down from the cockpit and walked away, getting their feet wet. A tractor showed up to tow the bird off to a hangar and the firemen began squirting water at the foam to disburse it. The watching crowd departed, most heading for McAllen and supper. It cannot be denied. Some of the boys were disappointed.

In the next several days, we all received orders to one basic flying school or another. Mine were to Laughlin AFB in Del Rio, Texas!

Three

Laughlin AFB

D EL RIO, TEXAS IS 320 MILES NORTHWEST OF McALLEN. It is
located in Val Verde County. The highway connecting the
two communities runs along the Rio Grande, passing through border
towns with fine old Texas names like Rio Grande City, Laredo,
Zapata and Eagle Pass. As Lieutenant Toof told us, Del Rio was
known for lamb's wool. We assumed this connected to multitudes
of sheep in Val Verde County. We guessed that the country
surrounding Del Rio was suited for sheep, and perhaps goats.

Except for a narrow strip next to the river, which was green,
the land was brown. Trees seemed stunted and, where there was
brush, it was scrub brush. The Rio Grande Valley, which was
green in Hidalgo County, turned brown north of Rio Grande City.
Strangely, though flocks of sheep must have been all around us,
in the six months we lived in Del Rio we never saw them. Nor
did we come across another local feature that was peculiar to the
town. It was a radio station, and undoubtedly a radio tower, that
specialized in broadcasting at night, taking advantage of the fact
that atmospheric phenomena allow radio transmissions to travel
farther at night than during the day. We were told that the broadcasts
were religious in nature, fervently hortatory in a style we sometimes

encountered in Texas. We thought we might catch the broadcasts on our car radio on the rare occasions we were out driving at night. But we never did.

Across the Rio Grande from Del Rio was a Mexican town called Ciudad Acuna. Compared to Reynosa, which catered enthusiastically to Texans and other Americans visiting Hidalgo County, Acuna was a conservative, inward looking town. The main square was distinctly old fashioned in appearance. A tired looking church and church buildings fully occupied one side. Sidewalks went all the way around. One expected to see mothers and daughters doing dignified strolling. The town appeared to have no commercial establishments offering goods for Americans. Land surrounding the town was dusty and poor. Many roadside dwellings had dirt floors.

Although Del Rio itself also was somewhat dusty and somewhat worn, my wife and I had better luck with housing there than we had had in McAllen. We were able to rent half a house, sharing it with a quiet couple from California. We had the front. They had the back. The boy was two classes ahead of me at basic flight school at Laughlin AFB. Our front half of the house consisted of a kitchen, a bedroom, a living area and a bathroom. Ample! There were several window unit air conditioners, not surprisingly all noisy and dripping. Because our stay in Del Rio was in the fall and spring, they were more than adequate.

None of the other Princeton boys who had been assigned to Moore Field with me were sent to Del Rio. My wife and I became friends with the California pair with whom we shared the house and, also, got to know other Laughlin AFB couples living in the same Del Rio neighborhood. With them, not long after we got settled in, we shared for the first time a sad experience that was not rare in the Air Force. Just as night flying had been part of the primary syllabus at Moore Field, so it was required of basic flight

A postcard showing the main gate at Laughlin Air Force Base, Del Rio, Texas, circa 1960s.

school students at Laughlin AFB. One evening a New England boy, a graduate of Northeastern University who we had found to be a cheerful new friend, married to a friendly girl and father of a baby daughter, went out to practice night navigation in the T-33. He was to adhere to a precisely delineated course. Included were segments to be flown at various altitudes, including low level segments. Somewhat drastic direction changes also were required. At one stage, within two thousand feet of the ground and in the process of making a relatively steep turn, the boy became disoriented, perhaps suffering vertigo. He may have confused down with up. Perhaps he mistook lights on the ground for stars. He flew his aircraft into the ground. The word the next day was that it impacted upside down.

At Moore we had observed the efficient way the Air Force dealt with washouts. At Laughlin AFB we learned the Air Force was equally efficient with death. Details of the boy's accident were not shared with student pilots. The boy's wife and baby girl were gone from Del Rio within a couple of days. At Laughlin AFB we did not march to class or to fly. So the death of the boy from Northeastern left no space.

Unlike Moore Field, which was a civilian facility managed for the Air Force by a civilian contract firm, Laughlin AFB was 100 percent military. As far as I could tell, it always had been. It had had its start in the middle of World War II. It came on line as an Army Air Corps training base, teaching boys to fly the B-26. The B-26 was called the Marauder. It was a fast, twin engine, medium bomber. In the beginning, it had a somewhat alarming reputation. Relative to the size and weight of the aircraft, its wings were small. The word got around: if you lost one of the engines, or if in some other way you lost power, the bird would drop like a stone.

Even a decade later, when class 57-M arrived at Laughlin, B-26 stories were told in Del Rio. One day at a grocery store I found myself in line next to a grizzled fellow who looked like he might be, or might have been, a pilot. His greeting to me was, "Mornin'. You out at Laughlin?" When I said I was, he said, "In the war I was an instructor out there. My main job was to keep the kids from killing themselves on those damn 26s."

****

Laughlin AFB had several runways. One of them, running north/south, was closely paralleled by a limestone ridge. When wind direction called for takeoffs to the south, B-26s were expected to clear the runway by making a right turn over the ridge. The old man went on, "Before they came to Laughlin, kids had been taught in the T-6 (the basic flying school trainer of the day) to pull the power back as soon as they cleared the runway. If they did that in the 26, after having taken off to the south, down they would go onto that ridge. A bunch killed themselves that way.

"To save my own life, as well as theirs, I had to break them of the habit. In those days, in order to talk on the radio in the 26, we used a hand held microphone. So I kept that thing at the ready. If a kid clearing the runway so much as made the slightest gesture toward the throttles, I would yell at him, telling him not to touch the power, and then I'd hit him a good lick with the microphone on the back of his hand. I'd save his ass, and mine."

At Moore Field, our instructors were civilians. They also were older men. At Laughlin AFB, our instructors were all Air Force officers. Many of them were young, virtually the same age as the boys they were teaching. Some of them were first lieutenants, outranking by one grade the second lieutenants they taught. Others were themselves second lieutenants, like their students. Some were a few years older, although even those fellows were only in their mid to late twenties. The individual teaching arrangement was essentially the same as at Moore. Each instructor had a table and trained no more than three students. Instructors and students were organized in units called flights. Each flight consisted of about a dozen instructors and about thirty students. Each flight had its own flight shack. Flight shacks lined Laughlin's main runway.

The commanding officer of my flight was Captain William Woodie. As many Air Force captains seemed to be in those days, he was a noticeably older man. I eventually realized that old fellows like Woodie were of the same World War II generation as our three Princeton ROTC majors. Their careers were not going to go much farther. Like the majors, Woodie's fond hope was to remain in the service until he reached retirement age. As he was well aware, occasional, brutal, money saving, housecleaning impulses would sweep the Air Force and the careers of old majors and old captains would be threatened. In the worst case, an older officer would be directed to retire early, ready or not. In some situations, older fellows would be given the option of remaining in the Air Force, resigning their commissions and staying on in enlisted grades. Reporting to Woodie at Laughlin AFB there happened to be one such fellow. He was a master sergeant who took care of parachutes. Only a year before he had been a major, even outranking Woodie.

The assistant commander of the flight to which I was assigned at Laughlin was none other than Lieutenant Toof !

My instructor at Laughlin AFB was one of the older first lieutenants. His name was Saul Waxman. He reported to Toof. He was a man of few words and, when he spoke, he had the sound of New York. There was an air of mystery about him. It was rumored *sotto voce* that he had had a serious accident. On final approach, at another Air Force basic flight training base, he had either come down on another aircraft or perhaps had himself been slammed onto from above. A few days before the accident happened, he had received much wanted orders to leave the training command and join an F-100 tactical fighter squadron in Europe.

The F-100, named Super Sabre and often called Hun, was one of the hot fighters of the day. Ambitious jet jockeys wanted to fly it. Sadly for him, Lieutenant Waxman's F-100 orders were cancelled. Although his Air Force days weren't over, they were at least detoured. Returned to training work, parked at Laughlin, his career was on hold. We never knew the full story.

Happily, the situation that undoubtedly was discouraging for him turned out to be beneficial for me, mainly because Lieutenant Waxman was an effective teacher. Although at first he had two students at his table, soon the second fellow took sick and was transferred out of 57-M. I then had the lieutenant all to myself.

Perhaps that was the luck of the draw or possibly there was some internal politics at work. Waxman was senior, a competent instructor and a well-regarded pilot. Possibly he had rights in Woodie's domain. And I may have been a desired commodity. If the standing I brought with me from Moore was good, Waxman may have said to said to Woodie, or Toof, something like, "If I'm going to be stuck here, at least let me keep this above average kid and spare me anyone else." The result was that I got lots of flying time, more than any other student in Woodie's flight.

In addition to Waxman, there was another, somewhat older first lieutenant with an unusual background in Woodie's flight. His name is lost to me now. But his face is not. He was a tall, extremely handsome man. He had high cheekbones, shining eyes and a straight, strong jaw. Without doubt the best looking man who flew for Woodie, he was black.

****

Even though President Harry Truman had integrated the United States military in 1948, the diversification of the Air Force wasn't very far along in 1957. The same was generally true of the academy in the United States. Although I had had black friends at the very forward looking boarding school I attended before going off to college, Princeton University during my years there was virtually lily white. Although one black man had entered with me as a freshman, by graduation he was long gone. No black student officers flew with me at Moore Field. Although that pattern repeated itself at Laughlin AFB, the color line there was not intact. This first lieutenant was there. And he was not just a student pilot; he was a full-fledged, rated pilot. More consequential, he was an instructor pilot, charged with and in every way responsible for teaching student officers all aspects of flying jet aircraft.

In Woodie's flight shack, his table was at the far end of the room from Waxman's table so I did not have particular contact with him or his students. However, very early in my time under the tutelage of Waxman, stories began to drift from the table where he and his students sat to Waxman's vicinity. They came in two big bites.

The ones in the first bite dealt with the fact that the black instructor's two student officers were from Mississippi. Quite soon it was said that the students were giving the instructor a hard time. They were resisting his instruction and demeaning him directly. He was handling the difficulty that this presented with composure. The second bite of stories concerned intensification of the conflict. It reached a point where the lieutenant was obliged to tell first one of the boys and then both of them that their flying was unsatisfactory. If pink slips were used in Woodie's flight, and I never knew if they were, presumably at this stage they were issued. The Mississippi boys then told the lieutenant that they were going over his head, complaining to Toof and Woodie.

The final bite of stories caused me and the student officers at the Waxman end of the flight shack who heard what was happening to applaud the United States Air Force. Because to their great credit, Toof and Woodie backed up the lieutenant. Not only that, they themselves got involved. They took the Mississippians up for checkrides. The lieutenant had recommended that both be washed out. Toof and Woodie, on the basis of what they observed in the air, confirmed the recommendation. Immediately thereafter the two bigots were gone. Good riddance.

The story has a puzzling end. Shortly after the Mississippians were dismissed, the handsome lieutenant was also gone from Laughlin AFB. We, the student officers at the Waxman end of the Woodie flight shack, were taken aback. Because we knew he would have been welcome to remain a Woodie flight instructor. He was well regarded as a pilot and as an instructor. We also knew there had to be at Laughlin AFB brass who would favor the lieutenant remaining with Woodie because they had backed up Woodie and Toof when they made the washouts happen. We could only hope that his transfer was positive in intent and effect. Perhaps it came with a promotion. Looking back, I hope that, in the happiest of outcomes, the lieutenant became a wing commander in Vietnam. Good black men did.

****

The basic flight school aircraft, as Toof had shown us at Moore, was the T-33. After the T-34 and T-28, with their piston engines, the jet engine of the T-33 at Laughlin took some getting used to. With piston engines, response to the pilot's throttle movement was immediate. In contrast, the jet engine of the T-33 responded only after a delay. This meant that, to put the bird where he wanted it, the pilot had to anticipate engine delay and, accordingly, make his throttle moves sooner. Also, flight controls in the T-33 were more sensitive. Steady flight required a lighter touch on stick and rudders. Landing speed was faster. Putting the T-33 on the ground required closer attention as well as a lighter touch.

When I arrived at Laughlin, and transitioned into the T-33, I was highly oriented to coordinated flight. Perhaps it could be said that I was preoccupied with coordinated flight. What this meant was that I had learned at Moore that the only right way to fly is to handle the controls of the aircraft in such a way that it feels just right. Movement of the aircraft is to be balanced and smooth. The body of the pilot tells him this is the case. Comprehension is often described as "what you feel by the seat of your pants." In coordinated flight, when the aircraft is flying straight, it is flying absolutely straight. This is the case whether the aircraft is straight and level, climbing or descending. It isn't flying sideways. It isn't skidding or slipping. The nose isn't wavering from side to side, yawing. Presence of those conditions is uncoordinated flight.

When an aircraft makes a coordinated turn, it is properly balanced in the turn. This means that it traces a smooth path in the turn, without sliding to the side, either awkwardly upward or awkwardly downward. To achieve this smooth path, turns are made using all the control surfaces: ailerons, rudder and elevator. Ailerons are located on each wing. They are interconnected. Raising one causes the other one to lower. Doing this makes an aircraft bank. Banking, the bird is ready to turn. It is the rudder and elevator that implement the turn.

The rudder is located on the tail of the aircraft. Like the rudder on a ship, turning it in the desired direction – the direction of the bank—results in the nose of the aircraft swinging in that direction. Unlike the rudder on a ship, however, the rudder isn't used by itself to effect a turn. Because, if the rudder is used by itself, it causes the aircraft not to turn but, instead, to slide sideways.

The elevator is also located on the tail. Raised or lowered, it causes the nose of the aircraft to rise or descend. Once a bank is established and the rudder is causing the nose to swing, the elevator takes charge of the turn, leading the aircraft to continue in the new direction the pilot has chosen. Simultaneously using ailerons, rudder and elevator, he achieves a coordinated turn.

The flight that results from these control approaches is called coordinated flight. In achieving and/or maintaining it, a pilot can amplify, or fine tune, the use of the control surfaces of his aircraft. He does this by using what are called trim tabs. These are small, supplemental control surfaces attached to the real control surfaces of the aircraft. Use of these tabs allows the pilot to enhance coordination. The condition of the aircraft itself, such as its weight distribution, or the unique design of its skin, or even the throttle setting chosen by the pilot, may mean that the normally useful position of a control surface does not result in the normally desired, coordinated effect. Slight movement of the trim tab on

The Lockheed T-33 "Shooting Star."

that surface may solve the problem. An experienced, skilled pilot always has the control surfaces of his aircraft trimmed. This means that all his trim tabs are in proper use. When I arrived at Laughlin, all mine were.

So my flying was smooth. But possibly it was too smooth. One of the errors almost every student pilot had to overcome on the way to becoming smooth was the tendency to over control. This might result from a heavy handed, or ham handed, touch on the stick or rudders. In doing away with the heavy hand, in my efforts to be smooth, did I become too gentle, even hesitant? Erring in that direction, had I risked not being firm enough, or positive enough, in managing the aircraft I was piloting? One morning, after a week or two of successful training flights in the T-33 with Lieutenant

Waxman in the back seat, he said to me, as we were doing air work not far from the Laughlin landing pattern, "Look, Lieutenant, you've got to make sure that you're flying the aircraft. You don't want the aircraft to fly you. It will if you don't watch out."

Although he hadn't said specifically that he thought I was guilty of letting the aircraft fly me, his message seemed clear. And that morning Lieutenant Waxman gave me a demonstration of what he meant by flying the aircraft. If I had a developed a tendency to be too gentle, or hesitant, the lesson he offered was intended to show me how to put that tendency behind me.

That morning I had been flying the T-33. Now Waxman took charge. As is customary in two seat airplanes where both pilots have a full set of controls (stick, rudders, throttle) and one of the two pilots wanted to take over from the other, he said, "I've got it." Immediately, unexpected things started to happen.

First, as Waxman said, "I've got it," beneath my left hand I felt the throttle leap forward, jamming up to 100 percent power. Second, at the same moment, the stick jerked violently to the left, putting the aircraft into a steep bank, abruptly tipped up on a wing. Third, these startling events were accompanied by a loud honking noise. Surprised, I realized it was the engine. I hadn't heard a noise like that before. In the short time I had been at Laughlin, jet engines hadn't been treated the way Waxman was now treating ours.

In jamming the throttle forward, he had kicked the engine in the ass. It was protesting. But it nevertheless did exactly what it was supposed to do, pausing for only an instant in its little delay then providing a burst of thrust that caused the bird to jump ahead. There were new lessons for me: when you need the engine to give all it's got, don't be afraid to demand it. Never mind gentle. Same with direction. If you need to get somewhere off to the left or right in a hurry, don't be afraid to rack it up and go. Suddenly I had a new idea: this is what fighter planes are supposed to do.

Where was Waxman going? For a moment I couldn't tell. Then another T-bird came out from behind a little patch of puffy, stratus cloud a few hundred yards off to our left. Apparently Waxman had spotted him before he had briefly flown out of sight. Now that he had reappeared, Waxman headed right for him. What was this all about? I would soon find out.

Barreling up to a position only thirty feet or so away from the other aircraft, Waxman began to cut his speed. The throttle came back a few inches and I felt the speed brakes come out, accompanied by their little wind noise, helping the bird to slow. Then the brakes were retracted and the throttle was advanced again, this time in small and medium size bites, some accompanied by honks. Waxman was advancing toward the other aircraft, closer and closer. I was an astonished spectator. For the first time, I was in a bird which seemed to be headed, deliberately and without question, on a collision course with another aircraft!

As we continued to approach, I looked at the two men who occupied its cockpit, one behind the other. There was a student in the front, staring straight ahead. In the back there was an instructor. He was looking casually from side to side. It was obvious that he had not seen us. Suddenly, looking back, he did. Surprised, he straightened up in his seat. Then, seeing that there were two of us in our aircraft and guessing that at least one of us was an instructor, and therefore knew what he was doing, he turned to say something to his student. If he hadn't already had the controls, he obviously now did. Making Waxman welcome, he waved cheerfully and politely held his aircraft straight and level so his visitor could fly close on his wing. Having another T-bird unexpectedly approach his aircraft apparently was no big deal. Seeing his wave, Waxman moved in even closer, closing sideways, making very small movements of the throttle and stick. When he brought our aircraft to a stop, we couldn't have been more than a few feet away from the other T-bird's wing. Waxman then said to me, "This is formation flying. This is what's called the wing position."

Waxman had opened a big door for me—in front of my staring eyes. And pushed me through.

He held that position on the other T-bird's wing for a few minutes. Then he dropped down below it, slid across underneath and emerged on the other side. Arriving there, stopping our sideways motion with a slight touch of ailerons, Waxman then lifted us back up to a wing position that was the mirror image of the one he had occupied on the aircraft's other side.

His T-bird wasn't flying him. Without a doubt he was flying it.

As we zipped quietly along, flying immediately next to the other aircraft, Waxman said to me, "Let me tell you about getting into position on another bird's wing. It's called joining up, by the way." He reminded me that Air Force aircraft have numerous, easily visible marks on their skin. He told me that a good way to get up close to another bird is to line up a particular mark out on its wing with another mark on its fuselage and then imagine a straight line between the two. Then fly up that line toward the formation position you want. The idea was to slide in closer and closer to the outer mark, the one on the wing, keeping yourself straight, headed in the right direction, by keeping the outer mark aligned with the inner mark, on the fuselage, as you approach.

Waxman started letting me fly formation the very next day. From the start, I used his joining up system. It worked like a charm.

Formation flying was such an important part of my Laughlin experience, and such an enjoyable part, that I remember only a few other things about basic flight school. One of them had to do with instrument flying. This term refers to flying in weather conditions. What is meant is bad weather conditions—mist, fog, rain, snow, sleet, cloud, storm—conditions that are severe enough to take away from the pilot normal references outside his aircraft.

He can't see the ground. He can't see the horizon. He can't even distinguish one cloud formation from another. As was once said, the world outside the aircraft is pea soup. In circumstances such as that, to manage his aircraft successfully, the pilot must rely on gauges, also called instruments, in his cockpit. The key devices used to guide flight are ones which show altitude, speed, heading and attitude. Attitude refers to an aircraft's orientation. Is it banking, climbing or descending, or some combination of those? The gauge that shows orientation is called attitude indicator. Other gauges present important engine and other aircraft system information such as temperature and pressure.

Flying in pea soup is called instrument flying, or, more formally, flying by instrument flight rules (IFR). Pilots wearing Air Force wings are expected to be able to handle instrument flying. So, in addition to demonstrating the ability in bright sunshine or on clear nights to successfully get off the ground, fly here and there and get back on the ground, an otherwise successful pilot candidate must show he can fly the aircraft in the soup. If he does that, he is considered IFR qualified when he is awarded his wings.

We got started on instrument training at Moore. I wasn't very good at it. Possibly that was at least in part due to the fact that Bob Joe wasn't very partial to it. Let's get this bird upside down! I did learn from classmates, if not from Bob Joe, that the best way to establish control over an aircraft in IFR conditions was to give greatest attention to the attitude indicator and the rate of climb or descent indicator. Keeping close watch on them, while also regularly checking the other gauges, would help a pilot make the movements of the controls that would keep the bird straight and level or, if necessary, return it to straight and level. So long as he was able to do that, the rest of the things he needed to do under IFR conditions usually could be made to fall into place. At Moore, practicing instrument flying was normally done in T-28s equipped with hoods, like convertible tops. They could be pulled up over the rear cockpit in which the student sat so he couldn't see out. He would have no choice but to do instrument flying, doing what was sometimes called flying the gauges.

At Laughlin AFB, instrument training continued. A few T-33s had hoods in the rear cockpit. I spent several hours under one and, eventually, was tested under one. I passed, and was considered IFR qualified, although I suspect just barely. One of the exciting moments in the instrument test occurred when the instructor in the front seat of the T-bird thrashed the aircraft around for several minutes and then left it upside down and severely banked in a screaming dive. It was then that he said to me, "You've got it." Having had the hood pulled over my head and thus unable to see out of the aircraft, my first challenge was to get the gauges to tell me what had transpired and what the situation was at that exact moment. What was the attitude of the aircraft? The maneuvers which the instructor had done were sufficiently severe that the seat of my pants would not tell me. Then I needed to use the gauges to lead me to bring the aircraft back to normal. Happily, I read the gauges correctly. Upside down, diving, banked. Then I let them guide me to return to straight and level. Success. The instructor and I had a laugh together.

Some of my Princeton ROTC classmates liked instrument flying a lot. They were good at it. They became accomplished IFR jockeys. Suggesting ultimate USAF wisdom, they ended up flying fighters in what were called all weather squadrons. Their job was to intercept and shoot down enemies flying in the soup. My eventual role also was to shoot down enemies. But bluebird days were my thing. I could at least hope to do most of my shooting in bright sunshine.

Another element of basic flight training at Laughlin was, as it also had been at Moore, navigation training. Because the range of the T-33 was more than 1,200 miles, and because the young Air Force instructors at Laughlin were more than happy to teach their students navigation on long trips to garden spots around the United States, most students were able to arrange extended cross country jaunts. I managed to make two.

One was with a first lieutenant instructor from Williams College named Keene Addington. In my father's words he was, like me, from a family of privilege. So he and I cooked up a scheme which would allow him to teach me navigation while by flying from dusty Del Rio, Texas to opulent Palm Beach, Florida. There we would visit with my wife's parents. We envisioned lolling around a beach club pool, sipping rum punches and ogling debutantes. What actually made the trip memorable was some of the flying. And our arrival at the Palm Beach airport was unusual. As was our departure.

Long distance flight in the United States, as airlines do it and the military does it, follows long established routes in the air. They were developed between World War I and World War II. Their original purpose was to guide the delivery by airplanes of airmail. They were laid out like roads, connecting city to city. They are called airways. When, under the direction of Lieutenant Addington, I planned our trip to Palm Beach, I looked up airways on a map, made note of a route, figured the time required at a given airspeed to proceed from one place to another and totaled up the flying hours needed to get from Del Rio to Palm Beach. I made sure, knowing the T-33's jet fuel consumption rate, that a full load of fuel would get us from Laughlin to the Florida gold coast with some to spare.

Our travel day was gorgeous in west Texas. I think in those years altitudes above 30,000 feet were reserved for the military. So we dutifully climbed up there and headed east. The only clouds anywhere in the sky were little puff balls way out on the horizon. The expanse of America that we could see from our 30,000 foot aerie was vast. For me, way, way up there for the first time, sailing serenely along, it seemed I could almost see the curve of the earth.

As we began to approach Palm Beach, after about four hours in the air, both Lieutenant Addington and I noticed that we were going to arrive somewhat later than planned and that there was less jet fuel in the T-bird's tanks than I, student dead reckoning navigator, had projected. In planning the trip the day before, back at Laughlin, I had checked on winds aloft the way I was supposed to. On the beautiful day we were led to expect, and had in fact encountered, not much was supposed to be stirring way up there. But obviously we had encountered a head wind. Perhaps the forecast had been wrong? Or perhaps I had misunderstood? "No matter," said Addington. "Just call up Palm Beach, Lieutenant. Tell 'em who we are, where we are, that we've got a little fuel problem and explain that we need a little priority."

One of the lessons to be learned in navigation training was how to use the radio and talk on it like a military veteran with strangers. So I set about the task Addington had assigned. After some fumbling, I found the radio frequency for approach control at the Palm beach Airport and made contact there with an authoritative sounding fellow with a big baritone voice. Somewhat timidly, I went through the suggested spiel. It didn't work. The approach control fellow said he did not understand what I had said and asked me to "Say again." I tried again. And again he said, "Say again."

That was enough for Addington. From his full, righteous eminence of first lieutenant, he took charge, forcefully stating on the radio that we were a United States Air Force single-engine jet with a fuel state problem in need of assistance. Suddenly the seas parted. Both of us heard on the radio the Palm Beach fellow tell TWA 3344 and Eastern 10 that they were to circle in place until further advised, that there is an Air Force jet on long final with a fuel problem and that their courtesy in giving way will be appreciated. So we flew directly in. At Addington's direction, I made the landing. As we taxied off to a parking spot, we saw TWA 3344 touching down at the far end of the runway. A great, big, four engine Constellation, painted red and white, full of paying customers, after us.

Sunday morning it was time to head back to west Texas. As we rolled onto the takeoff end of the active runway at 11:55 a.m., Palm Beach tower said to us, "Air Force aircraft please hold. Church services are still going on. Jet noise isn't allowed until after noon." So we waited, not releasing brakes and not rolling until midday straight up.

****

The normal quota of long cross country trips per student was only one. I happened to have a second one because my grandmother died. She was the woman who had kept house on the farm in northern Virginia. She was to be buried in a week's time in Richmond, Virginia. My parents, unable to get away, had called from New Jersey to ask me to attend the service in their stead. I had asked Captain Woodie. He had generously classified my inquiry as a hardship request. After a day or so, perhaps after bigger brass had been asked and had given a green light, Woodie had approved it.

It probably had helped that one of the instructors in his flight had a lady friend who lived near Richmond. So that instructor was more than willing to fly there with me. His name was John Ewing. Unlike Keith Addington, and me, he was no man of privilege. His parents ran a gas station in a little town north of Midland, Texas. He had scratched his way into the University of Texas. After a couple of years, he had quit and joined the Air Force as an enlisted man. With a year of enlisted service behind him, he had applied for and was accepted into the Air Force aviation cadet program that existed at the time. Graduation from that program brought him both his commission as a second lieutenant and his pilot's wings. Although Ewing couldn't have been more than twenty five years old, he was grizzled looking. He slouched. And he had a sardonic way about him. He enjoyed teasing ROTC officers for earning their commissions by watching movies. Like Addington, Ewing was known as a very competent pilot and a likeable fellow.

When I prepared the necessary dead reckoning plan, the final destination that I selected, at Ewing's suggestion, was, instead of Richmond itself, nearby Langley AFB. I guessed that Langley was closer to his girlfriend's place. Also, as the trip turned out, the choice of Langley was a fortuitous one. There was a radar system there that was helpful to us.

Because the distance from Del Rio to Langley was greater than the range of the T-33, it was necessary to plan a refueling stop somewhere on the way. On my map, Memphis Naval Air Station (NAS) appeared to be an ideal place. It was right on the route and about halfway along. With navigation done and necessary clearances granted, early on the afternoon of the day before the funeral Lieutenant Ewing and I climbed into a T-bird and set off.

A couple of hours later, as we dropped down toward Memphis NAS from cruising altitude, Ewing said he would be glad to make the radio calls if I would make the landing. This was an unexpected gift from him to me. He was offering a courtesy that normally only a peer would offer. I, of course, accepted his offer. As we slid down final approach, me flying the aircraft, the Mississippi River appeared beneath us, stretching off into distant mists both north and south, on either side of the bird. When a moment later it came time to think taking off power, slowing down and rounding out, raising the nose of the aircraft so it would sit down smoothly on its main

gear, I was surprised to see standing off to my right, at the end of
the runway, not many yards beyond the river bank, a man's
figure. He was black, dressed in a rough, work uniform. He had
a sailor hat on his head. He held paddles in each hand. At first he
held them out to either side, parallel to the ground. Then he
looked right at me, gave me a big smile and snapped the paddles
across each other in front of his body. An instant later, we
touched down. I said to Ewing, "Sir, did you see that Navy fellow
give us the cut? I guess he's a make believe LSO [landing signal
officer on an aircraft carrier]!" Ewing replied, "I saw him. You're
now carrier qualified, Lieutenant. Good for you."

When we had left Del Rio, the weather report for the trip had
been fair. But when we got back up to altitude after leaving
Memphis NAS, it was obvious that the rest of the flight would
need to be IFR. So we made the necessary radio calls, got IFR
approval and headed on. Our plan, based on the navigation I had
done back at Laughlin, was to use the ADF (automatic direction
finding) system installed in the T-bird to tell us when we arrived
at Langley. It was the most up to date, internal navigation system
the aircraft had. We knew we would get to Langley after dark
and, even if there had been daylight, we realized we could well
be flying in clouds and unable to see landmarks. So using ADF
was required.

The way an ADF system (today called RDF, radio direction
finding) worked was that the pilot would tune the instrument to
the radio frequency of the destination ADF station and, once that
was done, an arrow on an ADF gauge in the cockpit would point
in the direction of the destination and, also, make a reassuring,
confirming, humming sound. The pilot's task was simply to fly
the aircraft so that the arrow pointed over the nose. When the
aircraft arrived at the destination, the needle would jiggle, or
twitch, and the sound would stop. The new silence had a fancy

name. It was called the aural null. Some students, advised to listen for the aural null and watch for the jiggle, wondered if those instructions were for real. If the aircraft happened to proceed over and beyond the destination, while remaining on the compass heading that had been followed to approach the destination in the first place, the needle was said to obligingly swing around toward the tail of the aircraft instead of the nose. The humming would not resume, however.

In my dead reckoning navigation, as we flew on from Memphis NAS, I was able to project how long it would take for us to travel from there to Langley AFB and, knowing when, to the exact hour and minute, we had departed, I could forecast with precision when the aural null would occur. Because the ADF gauge happened to be located only in the forward cockpit of the T-bird, where I sat, I was totally in charge of documenting for Ewing and me that we had arrived at our destination. My calculations told me that the aural null would occur, and we therefore would be overhead Langley AFB, at 7:20 p.m. Eastern Standard Time (19:20 USAF time).

At 19:20, needle jiggle had not occurred. Nor had silence materialized. I said, "Sir, should we wait a bit?"

Lieutenant Ewing answered, "Yeah. Let's give it five minutes. Maybe ten. Maybe there was wind."

Both of us were well aware that our current heading was about to take us out over the Atlantic Ocean. Langley was on the east coast of the United States, we were flying east north east and soon there would be nothing but water in front of and beneath us until we arrived at Spain. The needle stayed steady as a rock, aimed at the nose. The hum hummed. Five minutes came and went. Silence from Ewing. Ten minutes. I said, "Sir?" He said, "Screw it. Five more then we do a reciprocal. You can practice your procedure turn." A procedure turn was a way of going back in the direction you came, retracing your path exactly in reverse. It involved turning forty five degrees from your present compass heading, holding the new heading for a specific length of time, making a precise, one-hundred-eighty degree turn, flying the reciprocal of the original forty-five degree heading for exactly the same length of time as used for the first forty-five degree leg and then, when that time interval was up, turning on to the reciprocal of the original heading.

At 19:35 no jiggle, no silence. So Ewing said, "OK. The damn thing must be bust. Turn it off. Let's head on back." I began to make the procedure turn. He then said, "My notes tell me Langley's got a pretty up to date radar deal. I'm going to call them and see if they can give us a steer." It didn't take long for him to make contact. When he did, he told Langley radar (I do not remember their official name) about our ADF problem and asked if they would steer us back to Langley AFB and Langley Approach where we could pick up Langley GCA (ground control approach). Their answer, "Glad to oblige, sir."

Ewing then said to me, "You want to fly it?"

I answered, "Now that we're not going to Spain, yessir. Thanks."

So then the radar fellow began to talk us down. His commands were headings and altitudes. Such as, "Turn now heading 180 degrees, descend and maintain 28,000 feet." At first, for a few minutes, we were in the solid soup. Then, when we were getting down toward 20,000 feet or so, the clouds surrounding us began to lighten. Next they started to separate from each other, leaving crevasses lit dimly from below. Great wisps hung down. As we descended, I made small movements of the stick, the rudders and the throttle, nudging the aircraft to follow the radar fellow's calm directions. We crossed valleys between clouds, returned to clouds themselves, slid through, came out the other side, passed down clouds' sides. The air was smooth and still. When we were lower, our T-Bird was suddenly in a big open space with clouds all around and bright colored lights, and white lights, shining up from below. It was a beautiful, unforgettable scene. Then I was in contact with GCA and they were bringing me down toward a landing, referring in their patient, guiding statements to glide slope, heading and rate of descent. At the end, they politely turned me loose with a kind statement I no longer remember. Undoubtedly they were politely saying that we were safely home and that I could do the rest. Which I did.

My grandmother's funeral service was held in a Richmond episcopal church. Afterwards, she was buried in the famous Hollywood cemetery in the city. Eminent Virginians and numerous Confederate soldiers lie there. One is my grandfather's uncle, who, as a Confederate lieutenant carrying dispatches, was killed by Union cavalry at a place called Roanoke Island. My grandfather's father, the dead officer's brother, and his grandfather, the dead officer's father, also served as Confederate officers. Both survived the war. As soon as my grandmother's interment was done, I grabbed a cab and headed for Langley. I changed out of my blue dress uniform into a flight suit in the car. Ewing and I needed to get back to Laughlin by bedtime. The next day was a work day. I remember that, on the flight home, Ewing told me to handle the required checking in with the various air traffic control centers that were located along the airways we followed going west. In the earlier cross country flight to and from Palm Beach with Addington, I had mostly botched those transmissions. This time I did better.

Once we passed San Antonio, night had fallen. The land we saw from altitude was black, black dark. Only occasionally did little car lights appear on the highway that ran west to Del Rio. West Texas is big, mostly empty country.

The next morning, as I drove out to Laughlin, a 57-M classmate pulled up beside me in his car. I thought he was going to pass. Instead, he stayed next to me, holding the shotgun seat window of his car even with my left, backseat window, only a couple of feet away. I yelled over at him, "Whatcha doin'?" He answered, "Flyin' formation." He only gave up his position beside me, where I realized he was playing wingman, when a car came toward us in the opposite lane. Probably he had his own Waxman. Probably they were a formation lesson or two ahead of the real Waxman and me. I would start catching up that same day.

Although it is lost to my memory, Waxman and his fellow instructors all must have followed a specific, step-by-step sequence in teaching student pilots formation flying. I believe I can construct at least a reasonable approximation of that sequence. But, before I do that, offering a sketch of what formation flying consists of might be useful. There are actually two formation formations. One is called echelon. The other is called trail. In echelon, a second aircraft, called the wing aircraft, or simply wing, closely accompanies and follows a first aircraft, called lead. The position of the wing aircraft is immediately beside the lead. In the vertical dimension, the wing aircraft is at the same level as the lead. Horizontally, it is only a few feet displaced from lead, either on his right side or on his left side. It is stepped back by only a few feet from even with lead's nose. The wing position is what Waxman showed me in his unexpected, ad lib lesson. Trail formation, and trail position, is simpler. In it one aircraft follows behind another rather than beside another. The following aircraft is said to be in trail. He flies only a few feet in the rear of the tail of the aircraft he is following. If he is following a jet, he positions himself a few feet below the lead aircraft's tail pipe in order to stay out of its jet wash.

Now about the sequence. My guess is that the first phase involved two instructors working together. Each had, in the front seat of his T-bird, his student pilot. The two aircraft departed Laughlin one after the other and climbed separately to medium height, perhaps 10,000 or 15,000 feet. There the instructors took turns joining on each other, showing what joining up looked and sounded like and talking the students through the needed stick, rudder and throttle moves. In my case, with Waxman's ad lib lesson already under my belt, I probably was encouraged to put my hands on the controls, joining Waxman to ease us over to the other bird. If that was the case, I also would have been urged to eyeball the two marks on the other aircraft so as to guide us moving in. A second step in the first phase probably involved switching from one wing position to the other. In other words, moving from one side of the lead to the other. Back off a tad, drop down, slide across underneath, stop, ease up, oooch over. Gently make the needed stick and throttle moves, and trim, to do all that. Just as Waxman had showed me that first day.

There was an aspect to properly handling the stick in a T-bird which I thought of then, and will always think of, as mysterious. Flying along straight and level, with the aircraft properly trimmed and the throttle setting fixed, the pilot could take his hands off the stick, and feet off the rudders, and the bird would keep right on doing what it had been doing, unchanged and unchanging, nice and steady. What was strange was that you could also put your hand on the stick and gently, slightly move it side to side— without affecting the attitude of the aircraft at all. No bank, no pitch, no nothing. In other words, there was play in the action of the stick. It was as if there was an activating button on either side of the stick, just a tiny distance away from center. If the stick was moved, but only within the play space, and thus did not touch a button, nothing would happen. On the other hand, if a button was inadvertently touched, no matter how earnestly and determinedly the pilot wanted the aircraft to stay steady, flying absolutely straight and level, whether he liked it or not, and even as he was certain he had hardly moved the stick, or not moved it at all, the wings of the bird would wag. So the successful formation pilot in the T-bird had to figure out how to play the play.

Until he mastered it, stick play could bite the student pilot. He might join up successfully. He would think he then was flying perfect wing. But his wings would be wagging. If there was an instructor in the back seat, that fellow would know. Whether the student pilot was solo or accompanied, lead also would see the wagging. One way or the other, the erring student would get chewed on the radio.

****

On a spring afternoon at Laughlin AFB, an echelon formation of four T-birds made a low altitude fly past to say good bye to a departing colonel. Extending airborne courtesy in this way was common in the Air Force. In this particular case, each aircraft in the four ship happened to be flown by an instructor pilot. As the formation flew over the head of the colonel and his crowd of well-wishers, which included a brass band, the wings of the bird in the two position, the aircraft flying wing on lead, were wagging. How embarrassed that instructor must have been.

Fortunately, I did not have the wing wagging problem. But I never was sure why I didn't. Was my grip on the stick just so sensitive, just so skillful? Or was it possible that only certain T-birds had the stick play problem while others didn't? Perhaps I never happened to get a bad one.

Early on in learning formation at Laughlin, we must also have been shown trail. In addition, we had to have been taught to effect a join up in echelon after takeoff. In this maneuver, the lead aircraft breaks ground first then undertakes a steady, gradual, climbing turn. His power setting is somewhat less than 100 percent. In this scheme, the wing aircraft after takeoff climbs after lead at full power, thus flying faster than lead, catching up with him and turning inside him at the same time. Wing's rate of turn would be slightly less steep than lead's so as to allow the distance between them to close. If the maneuver is properly done, wing simultaneously overtakes lead and slides up toward him. If wing is using Waxman's join up steering method, as soon as the needed two marks on the skin of the lead aircraft can be seen, wing begins to eyeball himself up the slope from the lower mark to the upper. When he then arrives at his desired wing position, next to lead, he pulls his power slightly back to bring himself to a stop—right there.

After I was shown the wing and trail positions, and how to join up, Waxman and possibly other instructors gave me practice time in my normal front seat position while they rode in the back. Then one of them checked me out in some way, authorizing me to fly formation by myself. There would no longer be an instructor in the back. Captain Woodie and his other instructors now were informed that I had been given solo clearance.

I say these things happened as if I remembered, although I don't. What I do remember are incidents that could only have occurred if I was flying in a sort of formation, fill in role in Woodie's flight. The context was daily practice by all the instructor/student combinations in four ship echelons, two ship echelons, four ship trails and two ship trails. I am sure I was never asked to fly four ship lead. But I do recall that I was assigned to fly both lead and wing in two ship echelons, in two ship trails, in four ship echelons and four ship trails. The flights I remember are ones when things went awry.

I am sure the numerous other formation flights that I flew on my own, where things went well, gave me pleasure. Including a puffed chest. How could they not. I was becoming a man among men, wasn't I? Although I still felt a touch of anxiety every time I climbed into an aircraft, my dutiful sense had begun to be accompanied, at least tentatively, by the idea that I was good at what I was doing. Maybe I was becoming a hotshot, or at least an embryonic hotshot. I didn't let my fellow students, or even my wife, know that this self-image puffing was happening. But for sure it was. And, in a perhaps not unexpected way, the flights that didn't go just right helped confirm it.

The first one of these happened with Captain Woodie.

One morning, as the flying day began, and Waxman had not yet arrived at our table in the flight shack, Captain Woodie appeared instead. He said, "I'll be working with Lieutenant Tanons this morning and I want you to fly lead." Lieutenant Robert Tanons, student pilot, was a tall, quiet Swede from the University of Nebraska or perhaps the University of Minnesota. I knew he had been struggling with formation. Perhaps Woodie was going to give him checkride? I couldn't help feeling sorry for him, having me along as both a witness and an ostensibly superior person, flying lead while he flew student. When Woodie and I walked out onto the ramp, two T-birds were conveniently parked there, not far from Woodie's flight shack. Tanons was waiting for us there.

After we were airborne, with Tanons and Woodie joined up on my wing, Woodie said on the radio, "Head on over to the acro area, Mills."

I answered, "Yessir. Rolls? Immelmann? Cuban Eight?"

"All of those," he responded.

So probably this was a fun flight for Woodie, getting the rust off after too much office time. Tanons was just along for the ride, allowing Woodie to log an instructor hour. I was relieved for Tanons. In a few minutes, we were into it. Woodie had dropped back from wing to trail and I was rolling. Somebody in Woodie's bird had a microphone open so I could hear grunting as we went up and around. Then I said, "Immelmann?" Woodie answered, "Rog." I was sure he was flying, Tanons just a passenger. As I came over the top and rolled out, back to straight and level, looking at a shining stack of clouds not far ahead of my bird, Woodie said, "You at 100%, Mills?"

He was asking, I realized with embarrassment, because he was having trouble staying with me. Probably he was embarrassed because of that. He also had Tanons looking on, after all. Obviously I had forgotten one of lead's obligations. It is to remember that the aircraft in trail, in order to hold its position on lead, especially when doing acrobatics, often needs to use a little extra power in order to stay close. To be able to use it, he needs to have it. With this in mind, lead gives up a couple of percent, flying at, say, 98%, so the trail bird, with 100% available, can use it to catch up if need be.

So I said, "Yessir, sorry."

"Try 98," he said, grumpily.

"Yessir."

Skirting the big stack of clouds, I led Woodie through a Cuban Eight, giving a figurative salute to Bob Joe as we went. Woodie this time was able to stay with me. Finally we did another couple of rolls and then headed home. I had been chastised a little bit about 100%. But that was a man's mistake and it deserved, and drew, a man's complaint, it seemed to me. So I lost no air from my chest. If anything, it expanded slightly.

The next slightly troubled moment occurred with Lieutenant Toof, of all people. One thing I tried to do absolutely every moment when flying formation was concentrate. I kept my radio turned up so I would not miss a single word. I responded instantly and precisely to instructions, whether spoken or signed, by hand motions or wing motions. And, when I was using the two marks on an aircraft's skin in joining up or when holding position, I gave them the continuous, constant, eagle eye. So it is with some wonder that I remember what happened with Toof. He was leading a four ship. We were either in echelon, all on the same side, or perhaps in trail.

I was tail end Charlie, either wing in the second pair (there were two pairs in a four ship, of course) or the end of the trail. Out of character, I claim—my wife had not had another baby—I was daydreaming back there. Instead of at the right level, I was possibly as far as six feet low, or maybe as many as ten. Lollygagging along. Suddenly Toof said, "Mills get the hell back up where you're supposed to be. You know where."

So, deservedly, I was chewed out. But notice the compliment at the end.

The third unwanted episode also occurred when I was tail end Charlie in a four ship. The plan was for three instructors with students and me, solo, to get out on the runway at the same time. We were to take off one at a time, then join up in pairs. The second pair would subsequently join on the first. The Laughlin runway we were to use was the same one the B-26s had departed then cleared from, turning over, or, on a bad day, onto, the ridge. Taxiing, we would approach it from the opposite direction of the prescribed takeoff run. At the end of the taxiway, we were to make two 90-degree right turns to get onto the runway. If one's aircraft had a handy steering system like, say, a car, this would be no big deal. Unfortunately, the T-bird didn't. The aircraft was equipped with tricycle landing gear. Each of the main gear wheels could be braked. Steering was done by braking one wheel or the other. The pilot did that by depressing the appropriate rudder pedal. The design of the nose gear wheel allowed it to swivel free. Its normal position was forward and back. In response to a main gear wheel slowing, or stopping, due to rudder pedal braking, the nose gear wheel would obediently turn. The problem was that too much braking could cause the nose gear wheel to turn too far, swiveling over to a position 90 degrees off forward and back. Once there, it would stay there—leading the aircraft to go 'round in circles or at least head off sideways from straight ahead. When this happened, it was said that the T-bird's nose wheel had been cocked. We were careful to avoid this, turning the bird slowly with little taps on the brakes.

On this particular four ship morning, as I made the second right angle turn, onto the runway, in a hurry, I braked too hard, pushing the nose around farther than necessary and managing in the process to cock the nose wheel. There I was, stuck, facing off to the right instead of down the runway, knowing that, if I continued, I would just keep on going 'round. In a circle. Disgusted, and sick, I informed the three instructors in front of me. One of them said, "No sweat. Just bounce it out." That was the USAF school solution. Put a lot of power on the bird, jam the opposite brake down to the floor, encouraging the bird to pivot away from the direction in which the wheel was cocked, get it rocking so that the wheel could turn and, Eureka, it would straighten out!

I tried. Without success. One after the other, two of the instructors took off. I tried again. Again without success. The third instructor called to say he also couldn't wait any longer. He then called mobile control, saying, "Starkey, I'm going on too. You better get over here and take care of this situation."

In a few minutes, Lieutenant William Starkey, instructor, drove up in a pickup truck and waved me out of the bird. I climbed down, helmet in hand, carrying my parachute. He got in my place and did what I had been too chicken to do: he ran power up to 100% and stomped hard on the left brake. Great clouds of dust rose up behind the aircraft and, as the Air Force expected, the nose began to bounce. That allowed the nose wheel to swivel and the aircraft to slowly turn left, straightening itself on the runway. Once it was properly aligned, Starkey taxied it away, rolling the T-bird briskly along with the canopy open over his bare head, taking it back to its normal parking place. At the same time, the Air Force pickup that had brought him out to the aircraft delivered me back to the flight shack. Getting out, I put my parachute down on the walkway to the shack, sat down on it with my helmet in my hand and waited for the sky to fall. Surely I was in disgrace. No doubt someone was going to come out and raise hell with me.

But no one came. After twenty minutes or so, I picked up the chute and helmet and took them in to the room in which they were stored. The sergeant who tended that place spoke to me politely as he always did. I then moseyed back to the table I shared with Waxman. No one was there. For an hour or so, I carefully studied issues of *Flight Safety* magazine, morosely killing time, waiting for the morning's instructors and students pilots to return from flying and the hammer to fall. In time they came in. When debriefings were done, a couple of boys said to me, "Let's go to lunch." No one, no student nor any instructor, ever mentioned my cocked nose wheel. Another Air Force gift, perhaps. Or maybe it was just the kind of little problem that even the best of pilots occasionally have. Not worth discussing.

Years later I happened to mention to a Princeton classmate my cocked nose wheel experience. He also had been an Air Force ROTC kid. He had gone off to primary flight school in Georgia not long after I departed for Moore Field. He then had attended basic flight school at Webb AFB, located in Big Spring, Texas, about 200 miles due north Del Rio. While I was the only Princeton boy in 57-M at Laughlin AFB in Del Rio and, as far as I know, the only Princetonian to serve at Laughlin, by some luck of the draw numerous Princetonians trained at Webb. I remember one of those boys, as snooty as the rest of us, telling me how amused he and his wife had been, when they first drove into Big Spring, to read a road side sign advertising a local restaurant which heralded "genuine West Texas cuisine."

Following up on our discussion, the classmate wrote this to me: "Your mention of a cocked nose wheel in the T-33 brings back unwanted memories. The condition was quite common, and it happened to me twice at Webb AFB. Practice there was to station two experienced instructor pilots in a shack located between the two parallel operational runways. They attended to observable problems with taxiing, takeoffs and landings. For instance, they could fire off a flare to send you around if you were coming in to land and the runway was obstructed or there was a problem with your approach. In the event of a cocked nose wheel, which usually occurred while turning to take the runway prior to takeoff, as happened to you, these two fellows would run out of the shack, themselves lift the nose of the aircraft and straighten out the nose wheel." He went on to say that he did not recall ever having been instructed to power out of the condition—as was the practice at Laughlin. I was tempted to tease him about the difference between the ladylike "let us help you" approach at Webb and the manly "do it yourself" approach at Laughlin. But I did not. After all, although I tried to do it myself, it was Starkey, not me, who solved the problem.

Flying for student pilots at Laughlin wasn't entirely all work and no play. On occasion we were told to take a bird up solo and just go fly around. Or at least that was the sense of the instruction; the actual phraseology must have been somewhat more formal. On one of those days I headed off for open country, planning to get down on the deck and do some buzzing. I well remembered an afternoon at Moore Field when I had taken a T-28 south across the Rio

Grande, over into Mexico. There I had eased down to tree top level and flown along blowing dust, ten to twenty feet up, hopping from one farm field to another. Entering a big one, I found myself headed straight toward a Mexican farmer on a tractor. Would I pass so close above him that I would blow off his hat? Would I hit him? I lost my nerve, pulled up right then, made a climbing turn, looked back over my shoulder. The farmer was shaking his fist. This time, in Texas not Mexico, in my trusty T-bird, I thought I would try again, staying down low and possibly blowing off a hat. Of course the bared head that would result wouldn't be that of a defenseless Mexican tractor driver. It would be an American's head. He would have rights. He could call Laughlin AFB, or the Val Verde County sheriff's department, or the Texas Rangers. Well, we'll see.

Headed toward what I thought was farm country northeast of Del Rio, I came across a nice flat stretch of stratus cloud. It lay as far ahead of me as I could see. Cloud buzzing was almost as much fun as land buzzing, in one way even more fun. Because you could get really low, almost touching the gray top of the cloud with your nose, reveling in the sense of speed as the diaphanous surface rushed by. The T-bird wasn't a supersonic aircraft. But it would buzz along at 400 knots and more and that seemed very fast when it was happening right on top of a cloud. Making a turn at that level, I tried to dip my wing into the cloud top, carving a long, curving groove. I then hauled the bird up and turned back, looking down, trying to spot the groove. But I had lost it—and suddenly the stratus cloud was left behind. Now the sky was clear ahead of me and on either side. And out on my right, not more than a mile away and only about a thousand feet below me, was, unexpectedly, a shiny bright aircraft. It was a T-28. He was climbing hard. What was he doing up here? Where did he come from? Was there a primary base nearby? Maybe Hondo? It looked like he had something in mind. His nose was now turning toward me.

A light dawned. This fellow's intentions were not friendly. Shit. What was I supposed to do now? In my time at Laughlin I had gotten pretty good at flying with people. I could put my T-bird right next to, or right behind, any other aircraft. And I could stay there, glued, no matter what the other fellow did. But I did not know how to fly against other people. My only experience was with friendly aircraft. I had not the slightest idea of what to do around unfriendly aircraft. If this fellow wanted to fight, as it appeared he did, I was at a loss. I was sure my T-bird could fly faster than his T-28. And I was still somewhat higher than he was. Would that suffice? Wasn't there more I should know? The T-28 was enemy. It was maneuverable. What are the fighting moves it can make? Can my T-bird match them? Could I match them? Suppose the fellow flying that T-28 had flown in combat in Korea, knew what he was doing, had tangled with MIG 15s, the jet fighters flown by North Koreans, Chinese, Russians? Suppose he had killed MIGs.

I decided to go home. I went to 100% power. Although I don't remember which way I turned, I know I turned tail. I used my bird's extra speed to leave that T-28 where I found him. I needed to be taught how to fly against an enemy.

****

At Laughlin AFB, class 57-M graduated from basic flight training in March 1957. A graduation ceremony took place at the base. Its high point was the pinning on of wings. March is warm in Del Rio, Texas. So the student pilots for the ceremony wore the handsome, Air Force summer uniform, the same tan with a silver cast that Colonel Ball had worn at Princeton six years before. The wives did the pinning. Once we received our wings, we were no longer student pilots. We were real pilots. The term the Air Force used was rated. As rated pilots, we were qualified, authorized and expected to do pilot work. If specialized training was required, and it usually was, rated pilots were considered ready and able to take it and succeed, without further ado.

Shortly before graduation, the Laughlin student pilots had been assembled for the announcement of class standing. At the same gathering, available next assignments were read out and the boys were instructed to make their selections in order of class standing. I was announced as first in the class. Numerous assignments at instructor school were available, as were assignments to train in B-47 bombers. Also, a dozen assignments were open for gunnery school in the F-84F fighter bomber. There was one assignment open for gunnery school in the F-86, the fighter aircraft called the Sabre that had taken on the MIG-15 in Korea. The school, where rated pilots learned to shoot, was located at Williams AFB in Chandler, Arizona. I used my first pick to take that assignment. I would come to think of it as another Air Force gift.

My reporting in date at Williams AFB was a week after graduation. So I remained formally attached to Laughlin for a few more days. I didn't do any more flying. I did spend a day in the role of officer of the day (OOD). As OOD, my primary duty was to greet, log in and offer guidance to visiting fireman, pilots and air crewmen who, during the day, flew various aircraft into Laughlin for assorted reasons. Some were simply visiting friends. Most were on official business with even more than the usual number of those types arriving on the day I served as OOD. This was because Laughlin AFB was about to be transferred away from Air Training Command (ATC), as it was then known. It would no longer serve as a basic flight school. Its training function, which had started with those B-26s during World War II, was coming to an end. As of April 1957, Laughlin AFB would be a part of the Strategic Air Command (SAC). It would be one of SAC's homes for the famous U-2 high altitude aerial reconnaissance aircraft.

On my OOD day, our official visitors included numerous, self-important, senior SAC officers, arriving in freshly painted, twin engine liaison birds. Much bowing and scraping was necessary. The most interesting SAC aircraft, however, was a simple and rather shopworn Gooney Bird. It had pulled up immediately in front of the little building where my OOD desk was located. As pilot and copilot, both captains, exited the aircraft, leaving the door open, I thought I heard dogs barking.

Once in front of my desk, the two officers said, "We are dog pilots. Notify your commanding officer that we are here." So it was SAC watchdogs that were doing the barking in that DC-3. Undoubtedly vicious, like everything else in SAC. Soon Laughlin would be surrounded by them. Newly arrived dog pilots, mere captains, could demand the attention of our commanding officer. Low key ATC days, with cross countries to places like Palm Beach, were about to end. I was glad to be going to Arizona. I felt for Woodie and Toof.

Four

Williams AFB

PEOPLE WHO KNEW WILLIAMS AFB referred to it as it "Willy." It always seemed quaint to me, and somehow appealing, that an Air Force base where boys were taught to shoot was called by such a diminutive.

The same instructor and table arrangement that had been in place at Moore Field and Laughlin AFB was in place at Willy. But there was a fundamental difference. At Moore, boys were taught one by one. Because the skills in the air they needed to acquire were practiced one by one. Although I had student table mates and shared Knox Faulkner and Bob Joe Carroll with them, I didn't do anything with them. It's probably for that reason that I don't remember them.

At Laughlin I was Saul Waxman's only student. I had no table mates. In the air, as very often the spare wing man, I flew formation with a lot of classmates but seldom with any one more than once. At Willy, I not only sat at a table with two other boys. I was being taught to fly and shoot with them. Once shooting practice began, I would fly with them every day. Because in the USAF the fighting unit was a formation, either the two ship or the four ship. Each two ship, otherwise known as an element, consisted of a lead aircraft and a wing aircraft.

In combat, the roles of lead and wing were distinct. Lead looked out front. He pursued the quarry. He was the shooter and, ideally, the killer. In contrast, wing's job was not to pursue or to shoot, at least in most situations. Instead, his primary responsibility was to protect lead's tail, sometimes called his six, with that term standing for the position directly behind, or at six o'clock on a clock's face. In order to do this, wing was obliged to stick with lead no matter what he did or where he went while, at the same time, keeping watch for enemies behind. It was this concept of the role of the wing pilot that made learning to fly formation, where flying connected to other aircraft was the essence, so important.

Necessarily, the great fighter pilot aces in our wars flew lead. The best of them gave great value to the work of their wing men. Usually, if a two ship was attacked, it would be the wing man who would be fired on first. Lead then would come to wing's aid. The nonpareils among leaders took pride in never losing a wing man.

Each four ship flight consisted of two elements, a lead element and a second element. Necessarily, each four ship had one boss. He was the lead pilot in the lead element. At Willy, at my table, the lead pilot in the four ship we three boys flew in every day was not only our boss in the air. He was our instructor.

My table mates at Willy were the kind of boys one might expect to rise to the top in the USAF. W. Scott Cooledge was a Harvard boy. He had been captain of the Harvard hockey team. He and his teammates were Ivy League champions his senior year. Douglas Dittrick was from Ohio Wesleyan. A scholarship kid, he had worked his way through college and played basketball for the school. Our lead, and instructor, was Lieutenant James Fox. He was a short, slender, quiet man. He had recently returned from Korea. Even though the war there was over, he had had opportunities to shoot at MIGs. He showed us gun camera film. Although in one

The main gate at Williams Field, shortly after World War II.

sequence it seemed he might have scored, the enemy aircraft was able to get away. As we came to the end of our days at Willy, Lieutenant Fox would urge us to apply for duty in Korea where, he said, we could shoot at people.

****

On our first day at Willy, Fox told us that the local inventory of serviceable F-86 aircraft was temporarily depleted. There had been a number of crashes lately. One was said to have resulted from a flame out on takeoff. The pilot was an experienced fighter jock who had only recently been transferred to Willy. He had done a good job of putting the F-86 down, gear up, in a farmer's field just beyond the runway. Unfortunately the field was bordered with an irrigation ditch lined in concrete. As the F-86 slid along on its belly, the air intake at its nose scraping up dirt, the chin of that intake impacted the concrete, causing the bird to flip onto its back and catch fire. Upside down with his canopy shut tight and jammed against the ground, the pilot couldn't get out and fire trucks arrived too late. In the same week, Fox added, two 86s had experienced landing problems and had taken the barrier at the end of the runway. One had caught fire there. The other didn't burn but was badly damaged. Fox didn't explain the landing problems and we didn't ask.

A few days later, when we had begun to find our way around at Willy, we learned that both pilots had neglected to insert and close gas caps on the wings of their aircraft, causing jet fuel to syphon out into their slipstreams once the aircraft were airborne. This necessitated aborting whatever air work had been planned. Returning to Willy after flying around in circles for an hour or so in order to dump fuel before landing and then touching down in a panic far down the runway, neither pilot had been able to get his bird stopped before running off the end, there encountering the standard USAF barrier fence. Taken aback, Cooledge, Dittrick and I said to each other, "There are pilots at this place that forget to put on gas caps?"

Because of the temporary shortage of 86s, Fox said, we'd do our flying at first in T-birds. "This morning," he went on, "the three of you can check out the area and get acquainted with each other in the air." So there it was. We were rated pilots. We were being told to go fly. On our own. So we had a little conference about how to use the radio, where we would go and what we would do. It was agreed that each of us would take a turn as lead and as wing in a two ship with the third aircraft flying along out to the side.

As it happened, when we arrived in the patch of Arizona sky where we wanted to join up on each other, I took the first lead. As agreed, Cooledge was off to the side and Dittrick was invited to join up on me and fly my wing. Wanting to be sure the area we were flying in was clear of other aircraft, I did a careful scan out front and then looked to my right side for Dittrick. He wasn't there. In fact for a moment he wasn't to be found. Then, on a hunch, I craned my neck, turning as far back as I could. And there he was. In a position that at best could be called loose trail. It was an awkward moment. I hardly knew this fellow. He had come to Willy, presumably, because he had successfully graduated primary and basic flight training, had been awarded wings and was a rated pilot. What the hell was he doing back there?

It then occurred to me, as I looked at his wretched wing position, that Laughlin must have done a better job of teaching formation flying than the basic flight school Dittrick had attended. Well, what's done is done. Should I now tell him where he should be? If we were going to fly the 86 together, did I have any other choice?

I am not sure what I said to Dittrick. But I do remember that I asked Cooledge to stay where he was and told Dittrick that I would now like to join on him, fly his wing. So I did that, putting myself right up beside him, tight on his wing, flying wing position as it was supposed to be flown. He looked startled at first and flopped his aircraft around a bit. But I stayed with him and he settled down. Then I went off and joined on Cooledge. For all I knew, his idea of the wing position may have been as correct as Dittrick's was incorrect. Or it may have been just as bad. In any event, he and Dittrick now both knew what I would do. They must have realized that they could do the same and probably should. Without discussion, they set out to mend their ways. By the time we first flew four ship with Fox a couple of days later, their wing positions were presentable.

****

Summer was fast approaching in Arizona. In the hottest months, the air in the afternoon got so hot and so thin that even Willy's runways weren't long enough for the 86 or the T-bird or any other, visiting jet aircraft to get off the ground. So flying was scheduled on mornings only. The day after Cooledge, Dittrick and I first met each other in the air, I was instructed to take a T-bird down to the bombing range that serviced Willy and get acquainted with skip bombing. I was told that a particular aircraft would be armed with skip bombs and that the sergeant who took care of the bird as its crew chief would show me where the bomb release switch was located. I don't remember who my informant was but I do recall that either that person, or the crew chief at the aircraft, explained that skip bombing is a low level deal so you need to be sure to get right down in the weeds. Did they realize they were talking to Mr. Dutiful?

Without too much trouble, I was able to pick up the compass heading that would take me from Willy itself to the bombing range. On the way there, I passed over a gray green carpet of some sort. Mindful of the low level encouragement, I pressed the T-bird down, leveling off just above the treetops or whatever the gray green layer was. As the bird and I buzzed along, I heard occasional bump-bump sounds. I was puzzled. Then my attention was abruptly drawn away from the noise by the sight of a mobile control tower coming at me on the left. As I rapidly approached, I was a little surprised to be looking up at the tower. But no matter. Where's the target for the skip bombs? Oh. There it is. Dead ahead. A wide cloth fence, extending out, side to side. Maybe the bombs tear holes in the cloth when they skip through? Pull the bomb release switch. Target zips underneath. Can't tell if bombs hit. Climb up and away and turn for home. Mobil control says, "Plenty low there T-bird. No hits." Flying back to Willy at 2,000 feet or so, no longer low level, it occurred to me that the gray green may have been the tops of mesquite bushes. Mesquite bushes! Six feet tall at most. "Fucking A," I said to myself, using a new term that seemed to be popular at Willy.

Once back at Willy, I parked the T-bird and turned it in to the crew chief. He graciously helped me out of the cockpit as crew chiefs often do. As we stood on the wing, chatting, one of his men came up, holding mesquite branches. "Where'd you get those?" asked the chief.

"From the lieutenant's wheel wells."

The chief grinned at me and said, "You were trimming mesquite."

"There was a bump-bump sound," I said. "Now I know what it was." We all laughed.

****

We flew T-birds for several weeks at Willy, waiting for the supply of 86s to recover. Perhaps we were waiting for boys doing gunnery ahead of us to finish up and move on, leaving Sabres available for us. I have only one more memory of a T-bird occasion. It involves a dangerous mistake I made flying second element lead one morning. Lieutenant Fox had taught the four of us to take off, and land, in formation. We would get off the ground in a four ship, the lead element, headed up by Fox, getting away first and the second element, led by one of the three of us, releasing brakes and accelerating down the runway a couple of seconds later. I think the interval was only two seconds but that may not be correct. Once airborne, the lead element would do the slow climb, slow turn that would make it easy for the second element to join up.

There was a lesson the three of us had to learn about flying second element lead during takeoff. It was to keep in mind that the way wing men fly is to instantly mimic the actions of lead. In formation, wing men do not separately decide to make changes. They obediently make them when lead makes them. The three of us boys, who would take turns flying second element lead, needed to have this in our heads. There was a particular moment in formation takeoffs when it applied. This was especially true if second element lead wanted to hot dog a bit by holding his bird close to the runway after pulling his gear up. Necessarily, tail end Charlie, the fellow flying four, following every move of second element lead, would also have his gear up and the two of them would be racing along, down on the deck, only a few feet off the runway surface.

Now the lesson. At this stage, both aircraft, gear up, would have wing flaps down. On both takeoff and landing, flaps were in the down position to give needed extra lift. It is imperative that lead delay raising his flaps a split second, as compared to his normal habit when flying solo, so as to take into account the fact that a certain airspeed must be achieved for a bird to fly without the additional lift that flaps provide and, in a two ship element, accelerating on takeoff, the lead aircraft will achieve that airspeed an instant before wing does. Forgetting this was my dangerous mistake. As I lifted the flaps on my bird, too early, I saw to my horror that wing was also lifting his, just as he was supposed to do. As he did, his T-33, not flying quite as fast as mine, was momentarily short of lift. It began sinking toward the runway. I was sick. I was sure his tail would scape the concrete. Then his whole fuselage would scrape then there would be fire and disaster. But, miraculously, he stopped sinking. God's gift of airspeed. He came back up to me. We climbed on out. Back on the ground an hour later, I did not mention it. Neither did he. It must have been Dittrick or Cooledge. Did he even realize what had happened? I never knew.

Aside from stick play, the T-33 had been fun to fly. Experienced pilots said it did not have bad habits. At Laughlin AFB it had taken us into the jet realm. At Willy it was available and accommodating as we waited for F-86s. But it wasn't good looking. What had Lockheed been thinking? Its nose was rounded, like the working end of the implement you spread butter with. The top of its tail was rounded. And its wings were straight. So it looked what? Inoffensive? Modest? Unthreatening?

Probably the T-bird could not help but suffer, in our eyes, from sharing the same space, Williams AFB, with the most beautiful of aircraft, the F-86F. The F model of the North American Sabre was the bird we would fly. The original 86, brought on line in the late 1940s, had been the F 86A. In the years since, the aircraft had been improved in various, technical ways and the F 86F was the most advanced version. In appearance the bird had never changed. From the beginning, it had been considered by most fliers to be the best looking aircraft ever made.

Perhaps understandably, it was said by some at Willy that the birds awaiting us there, having fought in Korea, were a little tired. They did not look tired to us. And when we finally got to fly them, they did not feel tired either. For us they shone. From the moment we first saw them we said to each other things like imagine being allowed to fly a bird that looks and flies like that and imagine been paid to fly a bird that looks and flies like that. For me, and I believe for Dittrick and Cooledge as well, and perhaps even for dry, quiet Lieutenant Fox, she was the beautiful Sabre. Was she a raptor? Or a shark? Or both? Sliced off, angled, shark nose, swept wings, swept elevators, raked tail and rudder. She looked beautiful and fast, even on the ground. She was profoundly beautiful in the air, ready, hungry, on the prowl, coming after you. Beautiful, dangerous Sabre. Even beautiful spelling. Sabre not *saber.*

****

On arrival at Willy, each of us had been given a thick booklet to read about the F-86F. Similar texts had been provided us at Moore and Laughlin for the T-34, T-28 and T-33. They were called "tech orders." They described the aircraft, its performance, its systems and the bits and pieces of those systems, in voluminous detail. In recent days, in the spring of 1957, we had been reading and rereading the F-86F tech order. Now, on a powerfully hot, desert dry Monday morning, we were told to spend as much time that day and the next in the cockpit of a parked 86 as we would like because later in the week for the first time we would be flying the bird.

We were about to experience a couple of firsts. We were expected to get familiar on our own, without anyone else's help, with the controls, the instruments, the switches and triggers, the ejection seat, the oxygen system, the radios and everything else in the cockpit of an aircraft we had not yet flown. If we had questions, we could go find someone and ask. But study time in the cockpit was strictly solo. We were rated pilots, after all. Also, when we first flew the aircraft, and ever after, no one else would be aboard. There is only one seat in the 86.

Two small rituals went with getting us ready to fly it. Those rituals told us, to our muted delight, that we were entering an elevated, special world. First, each of us was issued a different type of parachute. For the past year we had been equipped with a 'chute assembly which hung down behind our knees, suspended from straps across our shoulders. It was cumbersome. And dorky looking. The 'chute we now were given was a waist length, flat pack that rested on the pilot's back, like a jacket. Fighter jocks wore it. And it looked good.

Second, because flying the F-86F routinely involved experiencing elevated G (gravity) forces, as a result of the strenuous and occasionally violent maneuvers we would undertake, we were fitted with G-suits to allow us to successfully handle those G-forces.

G-suits are chaps-like garments made up of inflatable belts and leggings. Connected to a pressurized air supply in the cockpit, which automatically pumps air into the belts and leggings when the aircraft experiences G-forces, G-suits squeeze the pilot's waist and legs as the belts and leggings inflate. The higher the G-force experienced, the harder the belts and leggings squeeze. This squeezing beneficially retards the natural downward flow of blood, away from the pilot's head, which occurs when G-forces press down on the human body. With his blood still in his head where he needs it, in order to think and see, the pilot, thanks to the G-suit, is able to fight. Fighter jocks wore G-suits. And they looked good.

There were two other, sartorial aspects of flying the F-86F. They entailed wearing gloves and aviator sunglasses. Until I came to Willy, I had not worn either gloves or sunglasses. Although some of my student pilot classmates had, I thought they were an affectation. I did not see the need to protect my hands and the hard plastic Air Force helmet that I had been issued at Moore Field had a dark black visor which I felt sufficiently shaded my eyes. But Lieutenant Fox had told me that the elevated Arizona summer heat would cause my hands to sweat, and, as a result, possibly affect my touch. There were lots of touchable places: stick, throttle, trim button, speed brake control, machine gun trigger, bomb release, rocket trigger, radio buttons and circuit breakers. He also suggested my eyes might suffer strain behind the black visor. So I had tried both and was now converted. New 'chute, G-suit, dark brown, fine leather gloves with a USAF emblem printed on them and aviator sunglasses bought at the Williams AFB Post Exchange: I was ready for my close-up, Mr. DeMille.

✶✶✶✶

My recollection of my first flight in the F-86F starts with a friendly, soft-spoken fellow coming to Lieutenant Fox's table, where I happened to be sitting alone, and introducing himself, saying, "I'll be your chase pilot." Fox, Dittrick and Cooledge must have been doing something else that morning. The role of the chase pilot, when someone was flying a single-seat aircraft for the first time, was to fly in loose formation with the new boy, from start to finish of his initial hour. From that vantage point, he could provide by radio helpful counsel and/or direction, if needed. My chase fellow was a first lieutenant about my own age. I hadn't seen him before and wouldn't see him again. Although he must have been in some way connected to Lieutenant Fox, I never knew how. After shaking hands, I think we went out to the flight line together, climbed up onto a line truck and rolled along until we came to a parked pair of 86s which somehow we knew were that morning assigned to us. I did the required preflight, external inspection of my bird, including putting into place, and twisting tight shut, gas caps on each wing. He must have done the same. We each climbed up into our aircraft and spent a few minutes running through the printed, USAF preflight checklists that were clipped to legs of our flight suits. Probably the flight suit I wore was one of the ones I had first worn at Moore Field a year before. Did we then start engines at the same time? If we did, we may have agreed on the radio to do that. Or perhaps one of us gave the twirling index finger hand signal that I know we later used in Lieutenant Fox's four ship and was commonly used in Willy formations.

I do not remember if the chase pilot took off on my wing. What I do remember are the first words he spoke to me once we had climbed away from Willy and were cruising along at altitude in an area where air work was normally done by Willy birds. Up to that moment, the flight had gone like a dream. Taxiing the 86 was a piece of cake. Unlike the T-33, it had a nose wheel steering system. I think it worked off an angled projection of the stick. The device let us drive the bird on the ground like a sport car. Taking off was rapid. It even felt like the bird could have jumped into the air.

A three-ship North American F-86F Sabre formation during the Korean War in 1953.

Climbing out was the slickest of toboggan rides on new snow, only headed up. Response to my hand, my gloved fingers, on the stick was instant. Gentle touches brought immediate small movements of the aircraft. There was no stick play in this bird. Once I leveled off at altitude, with my chase friend in the same sort of to-the-rear and to-the-right, non-wing position that Dittrick had mistakenly occupied on the first day, which I took to be the proper chase position, I trimmed the beautiful Sabre to the point where it was flying hands off.

I looked out at the gorgeous blue sky and away to the Arizona mountains and began to wonder what to do now with this powerful sensitive responsive aircraft. As if the chase fellow read my mind, and undoubtedly I was not the first twenty-three year old to be so delighted with his first experience with an 86, he responded to my wondering, saying to me in a nice cool voice on the radio, "Would you like to roll it ?"

Did I say "yes" or "yessir" or "of course" or "absolutely"? One of those I am sure. I do remember what he next said: "OK. Just move the stick about an inch."

So I did just that. Just one inch. And immediately around went this beautiful bird. All the way 'round in a roll of its own design, completely circular, returning precisely to where it started, same altitude, dead flat, same attitude, dead steady, done. Pristine. Did I really do that? Did we, this amazing flying machine and I, do that together?

There are a number of different rolls. The names I remember are aileron roll, barrel roll and snap roll. There are others. I believe the roll I did, or my beautiful Sabre and I together did, in that magic first moment, would have been called an aileron roll. It is fast and scribes a relatively small circle. It is neither as fast, nor as violent, as the snap roll, which involves stalling one wing and the aircraft whipping around its fore and aft axis. I never did a snap roll. As compared to the aileron roll, the barrel roll is bigger, slower, more stately. Sometimes it is performed in segments, with pauses following each segment. There is a four segment, or four point, barrel roll. Perhaps there also is an eight? On that first day, under the spell of the one inch, first roll, I may also have tried a barrel roll. Later, on one of our last days with Lieutenant Fox, he led us in four ship echelon in barrel rolls. I was flying his wing. By then my relationship with the 86 was full-fledged romance. Concentrating intently on holding my position, hugging Fox's bird, with the earth slowly revolving around us, realizing we were together upside down, I found myself wondering how Dittrick and Cooledge were making out in their 86s. They were the second element. I hoped they too were succeeding. Because Fox had us doing the sort of flying that was the specialty of the USAF Thunderbirds acrobatic team. Were we, for a moment at least, as good as the best in the world?

When the chase pilot and I returned to Willy, we probably used a penetration descent from 20,000 feet and then what was called an overhead approach to landing at the airfield. Is it possible that one, or the other, or possibly both, of those methodologies had been employed at Laughlin AFB? I do not remember. So, for the sake of this paragraph in this memoir, I will assume that I was introduced to them both at Williams AFB. The penetration descent, which, as practiced by Lieutenant Fox, will be described in some detail a little farther on. As I recall, it was simple: if you have been flying above 20,000 feet and wish to go down from there to Willy, go to a place more or less above Willy at 20,000 feet, then put your nose down as steep as you want and dive like a bat until you arrive at landing pattern height which, as I recall, was at 1,500 feet. Knowing once you get there the compass heading you need to take to line up with Willy's active runway (the runway being used that day), making an overhead approach involves the following: approach the active runway on its heading at good speed, perhaps 300 knots; the moment you arrive over the end of the runway, called the initial point or IP, break hard left into a 180 degree turn (the turn is to be steep, perhaps 70 degrees; it's called a pitch out), take some power off so as to slow down, lower landing gear and flaps, descend; when the end of the runway passes behind the trailing edge of your left wing, start another 180 degree turn, continue to descend, line up with the runway, take more power off to slow to 100 knots as final approach speed, for landing take all power off, slow more, lift nose to round out, touch down.

Even if I had already made overhead approaches in the T-33 at Laughlin AFB, or in the T-33 at Williams AFB, or both, my first overhead approach in an F-86 at Willy, coming home from my first flight in that wonderful bird, is indelible. The steepness of the pitch out turn, moving the throttle back, the little roar of the speed brakes coming out to slow the bird, the rumble of the gear coming down, the little bump in the seat of the pants as the flaps come down, the decelerating then the curving, descending turn onto final.

As enjoyable as it was to do those things on my own, joy would compound as, soon thereafter, Fox and his three boys—he called his four ship Express Flight—would do them together. Every day that we flew, after doing a morning's air work, we would return to the airfield as a four ship, nicely echeloned to the right. Fox would pass over the IP first and pitch out. His wing man would count two seconds then himself pitch out. Second element lead then would count another two and pitch out and, finally, his wing, tail end Charlie, after a last two seconds, would do the same. So there the four of us would be, four beautiful Sabres aligned in the pattern, one after the other, slowing, turning, coming down, finally arriving on the runway at two second intervals.

Landing an 86, you touch down on the main landing gear with the nose wheel well up in the air. Soon enough, in the academy of the Sabre in which the USAF had so generously enrolled us, I learned something interesting about this standard, touch down attitude. It was that the elevated nose of the bird, suspending in the air the nose wheel, which normally, on its own accord, as the landing roll of the aircraft slowed, would gracefully bow down 'til the nose wheel joined the two main gear in contact with the runway, could be persuaded to delay this graceful bow. The result would be that the entrance of the Sabre, standing proudly and in grandeur on its hind legs, like the grand entrance of the pachyderms of Barnum and Bailey, was prolonged—to the astonishment and delight of those observing, presumably. It was on my very first landing as Express Flight lead element wing that I discovered the following secret method of causing such a delay, to this day not technically understood: as soon as the main gear touch down, with the nose in the air, run elevator trim to maximum forward.

As my bird continued on with its nose in the air, I noted with satisfaction that the nose wheels of second element lead and his wing, both behind me, one by two seconds and the other by four, were both down on the concrete. They were handling the controls of their birds in the conventional way. I was doing something different. The result could be seen. Their noses were down. Mine was still up.

As soon as I had a moment alone at the table with Dittrick and Cooledge, I briefed them. Listening politely to my description of my discovery and gracefully responding to my invitation to cooperate in its exploitation, they agreed to join me in running elevator trim maximum forward the next time they touched down. They did and, sure enough, it worked perfectly. There was Lieutenant Fox with his nose down on the runway in usual style with the three of us following with all of our noses in the air. Our delight was unbounded. At the conference of the three of us around the table that ensued, we pondered how best to take advantage of our new found capability. We decided to proceed, without hesitation, to the next level. We would not only hold our noses in the air as we rolled straight down the runway. We would make every effort to also keep them suspended as we turned off the runway, thus arriving on a Willy taxiway on two wheels. Observers would be astounded. The feat would be stuff of legend.

The very next day, the opportunity presented itself. Lieutenant Fox had turned off. On all three wheels, as usual. I was two seconds behind, still on two wheels, nose high. As I approached the turn, mobile control unexpectedly spoke in my ear on the radio, "Express Two better put that nose down. Not sure the bird is built to handle going around corners on two wheels." Triumph and despair in the same moment. Mobile control, with who knows how many fly boys also in attendance, was watching. An audience! Obviously they had watched us today and, for all we knew, on prior occasions as well. Not just any audience. A knowledgeable one! At the same time, it was clear the jig was up. Although our caper may have been unique in F-86F history, its moment had come and, also, gone. The USAF would not risk breaking the bird.

****

The air work we were doing was of a serious nature. An early Express Flight assignment was dive bombing. As I remember it, the bombing range was next door to the skip bombing target that I had attacked unsuccessfully at mesquite bush level at the start of my Willy days. Dive bomb targets were big, concentric circles marked in lime on the ground. What we carried as bombs were bags or boxes of white powder. They would make a clearly visible splash when they hit, allowing us to see if we had connected with the target. On each flight to the bomb range, we made a number of bomb runs. In all the runs I did, I only hit the target once or twice. Possibly I didn't have my bird in quite the right position when I released my bombs, although I found the process of getting organized to make the drop to be appealing and believed I was proceeding correctly. Express Flight would arrive at the range as a four ship. We would then follow each other to the target on agreed upon compass heading, altitude and airspeed, separated from each other by agreed upon seconds.

What we did when we got close to being directly above the target was the fun part. As soon as the limed circles passed under the left wing, we would roll onto our back, then pull the nose down to the vertical. At that moment the target would appear off our right wing. Then, to align with it, we would roll 90 degrees to the right, putting the target on our nose. We would then dive toward it and, at a moment now forgotten, release the make believe bomb. Some years later, I described this maneuver to my wife's uncle, who had been a pilot in the United States Marine Corps in World War II. He had flown a Douglas Dauntless dive bomber out of Guadalcanal. He had many times bombed Japanese positions. After hearing me out, he smiled and said, "You sure wouldn't have done all that rigmarole in combat. If you had, the Japs would have gotten a bead on you in the first few seconds and shot your ass off." I asked him how real bombing was done. He said, "Get close to the target, dump your nose, drop that thing and get the hell out of there. Never mind all that rolling and turning."

****

Our 86s also carried rockets. In practicing with them, I think the three of us echeloned off to the right of Fox and in some fashion took turns shooting from that formation. Our targets were surplus military airplanes, parked out in long rows in the desert. I remember recognizing World War II bombers, B-17 Flying Fortresses and B-24 Liberators. Did we use the gunsight in our cockpit when we shot rockets at them? Or were we low enough, and close enough, that we just generally pointed our birds and fired away? I do remember Cooledge saying to me on the radio, "Good shot, three. You blew his wing off." Was it one of the specially designed B-24 wings, which in theory allowed the Liberator to fly faster? Did I see the wing I hit fly up in the air, spinning? I don't think so. For some reason, I think only Cooledge saw it.

I believe in 1957 Williams AFB was one of only a few USAF bases in the Lower 48 where gunnery was being taught. Nellis AFB in Nevada and Luke AFB, in Glendale, Arizona, were others. Two of my Princeton Air Force ROTC classmates were training at Luke at the same time that I was at Willy. Unfortunately for them, the aircraft they flew at Luke wasn't the well-liked and respected F-86. It was the F-84F, officially named Thunderstreak and tellingly called "hog." A swept-wing version of the original, straight-wing F-84 that had flown air to ground missions in Korea, the F-84F was known to be a troubled bird. Its accident record at Luke was not good. Both of the Princeton boys suffered accidents. One, on his first flight in the F-84F, crashed the bird on landing. In the investigation that necessarily ensued, he was judged to be at fault, stripped of his wings and sent to serve out his USAF tour as a ground pounder at a radar station.

The other Princeton fellow had his engine come apart at altitude, causing the bird to flail about, throwing him around in the cockpit, his helmeted head banging against the Plexiglas canopy. He successfully activated his ejection seat and was automatically separated from it, finding himself drifting down toward the desert under his parachute. He remembered being taught at either primary or basic flight school that parachutes can be steered by pulling on the risers that connect the pilot to the canopy above. So he tried it. He was horrified to see the canopy, in response to his tugging, start to collapse. Enough of that!

No longer tugging, with the canopy of his 'chute returning to normal, he calmed down. He found that the trip to earth was going slowly. To pass the time, he took his credit cards out of his flight suit pocket and separated out the ones that were out of date. Unlike the other Princeton boy, he was judged not to be at fault. He managed to complete the Luke course and escape to an F-86F squadron in Korea.

Visiting firemen would appear at Willy. Fighter pilots from throughout the USAF enjoyed doing the things that were done there. One morning a tall, dark haired major who was the spitting image of Randolph Scott, and who must have been a World War II flier, showed up at our table in place of Lieutenant Fox. Later, the three of us tried to call his name but couldn't. He took us bombing. When we arrived at the range, mobile control advised us that something was being done at the west end. So we were instructed to recover from our drops by turning left instead of right as we usually did. I was flying second element lead with Dittrick on my wing. I went through the customary gyrations preparing to dive, admiring the peerless precision of my rolling. I dropped my bomb, saw a hit, patted myself on the back and recovered by turning right. I immediately heard Dittrick say, "Ahem" on the radio. Very tactful. Then the major added, "Wrong way, Lieutenant." No further discussion was required nor ensued. In the company of men, just another cocked nose wheel.

The room in the flight shack where the table of Express Flight was located had two levels. Senior types, including visitors, sat on the upper level, a couple of feet above the rest. Late one morning, when Lieutenant Fox and the three of us were talking after flying, still in our flight gear, I noticed a bird colonel in a flight suit drinking coffee at a table on the upper level. I couldn't help but stare at his feet. He wasn't wearing the boots the rest of us wore. He wore moccasins and white socks. He was an older man, big, handsome. From time to time he turned and looked down at us. I recognized him from World War II photographs. Colonel Donald James Matthew Blakeslee. He flew the Spitfire, the Thunderbolt and the Mustang in the big war. He got his first kill in a Spitfire in 1941, having joined the Royal Canadian Air Force when American wasn't yet in the war. In 1942, he switched to the U.S. Army Air Force. By the war's end, he had 15.5 kills in the air and two more on the ground. He flew more combat missions against the Luftwaffe than any other American fighter pilot. He later flew in Korea. It occurred to me that the Air Force probably allowed him to wear any footgear that he wanted. Perhaps, at some point in his many hours of combat flying, his aircraft had been hit, there had been fire and his feet had been burned. So boots would hurt. I couldn't help wondering if the boys he was looking down at reminded him of boys he had flown with in war.

****

One day at Willy I was invited to fly for an hour or so in the back seat of a T-33. I had never been in that seat before. As a student pilot at Moore and Laughlin, I always flew in the front, either with an instructor in the back or when I was alone. As a rated pilot at Williams, when I flew the T-33 I always had the bird to myself and, accordingly, flew in the front. My little mission in the back seat was to be somewhat unusual. The aircraft was going to tow behind it, on a long length of cable, a rectangular canvas sleeve that was the target for F-86 pilots learning air-to-air gunnery. My job was to keep a close watch on the boys who were trying to hit the sleeve with 50-caliber machine bullets. If they were flying their pattern correctly, when they were shooting at the sleeve they would be approaching it at an angle. The course of their bullets would therefore not be aligned with the flight path of the tow plane. The slugs would safely pass well behind it. A common beginners' error in air-to-air gunnery, however, was to wait too long to shoot, thus flattening out the firing pass and shooting at the sleeve not at an angle but from behind. Obviously this could result in bullets not necessarily passing safely behind the tow plane but, instead, approximating, if not actually tracking, its direction of flight. This might result in slugs up the tow plane's tailpipe, into its fuselage or even into it cockpit. My job was to watch out for this possibility, warn the tow pilot if it seemed imminent, alerting him to raise hell with the shooters and, in the worst case, to cancel the exercise altogether by cutting loose the cable and sleeve.

What made this watch dog mission even more interesting, the day I happen to fly it, was that the four ship that was going to be shooting consisted of one dependable American fighter pilot instructor as flight lead and three Korean pilots as wingmen. In 1957, nobody at Willy had much use for Koreans in general or Korean pilots in particular. Pilot training in Korea was thought to be sketchy. Many graduates were judged to be inept, or undisciplined, or both. It was widely thought that, if shooting up a tow plane from the rear were to be done, it would be Koreans who would do it.

Nonetheless, their country was our country's ally. So, apparently without complaint at higher levels, we taught gunnery to their pilots. As the tow plane pilot and I had climbed into the bird, the crew chief who tucked us in wore a big smirk and muttered something about chop suey. But, all the fretting notwithstanding, the exercise came and went without incident. Although the flight was late in arriving at the perch and ragged in its sequence of firing passes, there had been nothing unsafe about what either the instructor or his Koreans had done. We had no problems to report. To no one's surprise, though, none of the Koreans had managed to hit the target. But most Americans at Willy had that problem too.

A couple of days later Dittrick, Cooledge and I were reminded again of the big war. And new allies. We were standing on the flight line, waiting for a line truck to take us to our birds. It was early morning as it usually was when we were flying in the summer at Willy. When a truck stopped in front of us, we saw that there were three men already in it. They wore dark blue flight suits. We hadn't seen flights suits like that before. The men were tall, dark haired but graying, handsome. They were speaking German. As the three of us clambered up and took our seats on the benches that lined the sides of the truck bed, the Germans stood up. There was more than enough room in the truck for the six of us. They had not needed to stand.

They looked to be in their early thirtiess. They were old enough to have flown in World War II. Little more than a decade earlier. Did they stand for us out of respect? Or enmity? Did we remind them of American boys they had fought? I was rattled by them, by their composure. Awkwardly, I said to my colleagues, "How about that. Real fighter pilots. Luftwaffe." The Germans heard. They stared at us and we stared back. The truck stopped at our 86s and we got off. As we walked to our aircraft, we wondered if we might be flying with those Germans someday, or perhaps against them.

From time to time, Lieutenant Fox and his three boys would discuss at the Express Flight table emergency procedures. Also, each of the three of us, on our own initiative, would spend time reviewing the F-86 tech order, which dealt with problems which could occur on the F-86 and spelled out recommended solutions. Fortunately, in our days at Willy, unlike my Princeton classmates at Luke with the benighted F-84F, we didn't encounter major difficulties. But both Cooledge and I did experience minor problems. Mine will be described a little later. Cooledge's happened one morning when the four of us were coming home from doing air work. Fox had his own, special way of getting back down from altitude to the Willy landing pattern. Starting at 20,000 feet, or whatever height we happened to occupy at altitude, he would tell to us to switch from echelon to trail. The telling was done either with a wing wag or a hand signal. To the extent possible, as was the USAF custom in combat, we had done away with radio talk. At the most, radio clicks were used. With the three of us repositioned in trail, perhaps as confirmed by each boy with a click, Fox would get onto his back, pull his nose down and start rolling toward the deck. Each of us would follow suit. I often wondered what a sight we must have made. Four beautiful Sabres, nose to tail, headed straight down, all rolling round and round, aimed for the deck. As he approached landing pattern height, Fox would signal us to switch back to echelon, level off and start slowing down, reducing power and deploying his speed brakes. As each of us followed his lead, flattening out, we too would put out our brakes to decelerate as we eased back into echelon.

I happened to be flying Fox's wing that morning and Cooledge, as second element lead with Dittrick on his wing, was due to join up on me as we headed for the landing pattern. So I was the first, other than Cooledge himself, to realize that second element lead had a problem. This was because Cooledge, instead of scootching up to my wing as was his habit when the Fox vertical rolling circus came to an end, had gone barreling right by and now found himself out front of the flight, fast leaving us behind. In a quiet, entirely composed, voice, he used the radio, as only made sense under the circumstances, saying, "No brakes." And then, "Using the hand crank." What a cool cat our Harvard hockey captain proved himself to be. Not only did he not sweat the loss of his speed brakes. He remembered the applicable emergency procedure and implemented it. And then, when he had gotten his brakes deployed, he dropped his bird down, backed it up and joined on me, with Dittrick then joining on him, as if that was the way we always got ready for our overhead approach at Willy.

On some days, in the course of gunnery training, we were sent off on our own in those beautiful Sabres to do whatever we wanted to do. We could go practice something or explore or whatever. We were all aware that the F-86 was described as a supersonic aircraft. Accordingly, in the cockpit of each one there was an instrument denominating airspeed not in miles per hour or knots but in terms of Mach, Mach 1 being the speed of sound, Mach 2 being twice the speed of sound, et cetera. Because the speed of sound varies with the temperature of the air, generally speaking it is higher at warmer, lower altitudes than at colder, higher altitudes. We were told that the 86s we were flying, when they were brand new, could exceed the speed of sound at sea level in level flight. Now that they had some hours on them, we were told it would be necessary to point them straight down to achieve that speed.

So a number of us went out to lightly inhabited places, where the sonic boom wouldn't be too bothersome, and did just that. As I watched the Mach needle pass through 1, I half expected trumpets to blow in celebration or, at the other extreme, some sort of control surface stiffening to occur. One of the Air Force majors at Princeton had said in military science class that P-47 Thunderbolts, Lieutenant Toof's jugs, had severe, and sometimes fatal, control problems when they approached the speed of sound.

But, because, with its handsome swept wings, it was made for supersonic flight, absolutely nothing happened in the beautiful Sabre. There was no sensation. One moment we were slower than sound. The next moment we were faster. It if hadn't been for the Mach instrument, I wouldn't have known the difference.

As flat as going supersonic was, an exploration on another day was wildly dramatic. In an unexpected way, the experience was magnificent.

What I had set out to explore was the sky above, asking the beautiful Sabre how high she could go. The first part of the trip was familiar. Throttle at 100%, nose up, gradually rising. That day there were clouds here and there. So, on the way up, there were great, white headlands and billowing towers to circumnavigate. That made much of the steady climb glorious sightseeing, reminiscent of the beautiful night descent into Langley AFB in the T-bird the year before. Once in a while, as the Sabre and I rose, moving above 30,000 feet, I saw other aircraft down below, curving around cloud faces or darting in open spaces.

At about 45,000 feet we left the clouds behind. I began to notice a sort of hesitancy in the bird's upward movement. Then there was something else up there that was extraordinary. And hugely compelling. It was the color of the sky. Until that moment, to the extent that I had ever given serious thought to the color of the sky, I had assumed blue. Blue is what is observed from earth. Blue is wild blue yonder. Blue is what I had seen from every airplane I had ever ridden and from every aircraft I had ever flown. But now, above the beautiful Sabre and me, was a great vault of a totally different color. It was black. Was this the real sky and, if it was, where was blue? Then, in an instant, I had a change of heart. Let's skip the questions. Let's just assume it's magic. Down there it is blue, up here it is black. I had been blessed to see both.

The beautiful Sabre was willing to go a little farther, but not much. At 47,000 feet, she began to feel as if she was on ice. Sliding. Slipping. She would gain another foot, or perhaps only another six inches, and then lose what she had gained. And then she would lose some more. Why? Well, the air is very thin. But is it uneven in its thinness? Are there pockets that are thinner than other pockets? Were we moving from one to another? Not knowing, in the seat of my pants I began to feel that we were on the edge of a cliff. About to go over. Anxious. Maybe it would be best if I were to quit asking for more height. So I stopped trying to climb and let the 86 come down, wishing that the feeling that we were about to fall would go away. After a while it did and I was relieved although, back amongst clouds, I was already mourning the loss of black and, even, grieving a little bit that my beautiful Sabre was no longer skating.

We were taught some things at Willy that were so much fun for twenty-three-year-old boys. At a threshold level, we were delighted with the responsiveness and grace of the F-86F. Imagine what went through our heads as we listened to Lieutenant Fox tell us, in so many words, that this morning we will get into beautiful Sabres, fly them out into the desert, there get down on the deck as Express Flight and do authorized buzzing. Of course this wasn't exactly what Lieutenant Fox said. Without even a touch of irony, what he actually said was, "This morning we will familiarize you gentlemen with low-level flight; we will get down low enough to herd wild horses." Amazing.

First, did the Air Force really assume that rated pilots who had made it to gunnery school had never on their own gotten down on the deck and buzzed? Threatening Mexican farmers for example? Even I, tending toward goodie-goodie, had done that. Second, were we really going to chase wild horses?

Somewhat stunned, we strapped on our G-suits, shaded ourselves with aviator glasses, ducked into our hard plastic helmets and went off to pursue mustangs and their consorts with fighter planes. As best we could tell, the location where the horses were to be found was Fox's secret. It was a canyon that abruptly appeared as a gouge on the surface of a desert plateau somewhere west of Willy. It was carpeted in green grass, perhaps explaining the horses' residency. At its entrance it was wide enough to accommodate the four 86s of Express Flight in echelon. As soon as we got down on the top of the grass, with throttles pulled back so as to slow toward horse herding speed, we could see the creatures up ahead. Perhaps accustomed to visits from Fox, they had already turned away from us. So on we came at horses' ass level. Even as slow as we were going, the herding didn't last long. Pulling up and over the beasts, we headed for the wild blue.

Another lesson that might have been offered at Willy at negative cost (we would have paid) was shooting at things on the ground from the beautiful Sabre with machine guns. In addition to the horses' canyon, there were lots of cracks and crannies out in the desert and at least a couple of them contained things we were authorized to shoot at. Putting targets in such locations I suppose simulated efforts by enemies to shelter their hardware from attackers like 86s.

At Willy, when we were shooting machine guns, it was customary to load bullets in only one of the six 50-caliber weapons that the F-86F carried. We were just learning to hit things, not learning to destroy them. And, after all, it was peace time.

Although in earlier parts of this memoir I have told about dropping bombs and firing rockets from the 86, I have no recollection of how, or where, those things got attached to the bird so we could drop or fire them. In contrast, I do remember how our machine gun was loaded. On the way out to the takeoff end of the active runway, the four of us in Express would stop, one at a time, at an armorers' station. It must have been a trailer of some kind. As the enlisted man who was loading the gun appeared at the nose of each aircraft to do his work, the pilot was required to put his hands up on the canopy rail where they could be seen. Obviously this was a safety precaution, ensuring that the pilot did not touch the trigger and inadvertently fire the weapon as it was being readied. This contact between pilot and armorer seemed to me a special, exclusive ritual of the fighter pilot tribe, like flying the 86 itself. Once, as I put my own gloved hands out on the canopy rail where they could be seen, I thought of James Jones's book, *From Here to Eternity*. In the peacetime Army in Hawaii, just before the big war, Jones's character Prewitt had especially loved working with machine guns, taking them out onto the range, setting them up, feeding them, firing them, taking them down, cleaning them. That morning I would have my own machine gun experience. I remember it, and the shooting occasions that followed, fondly.

The targets parked partially hidden in crevasses out in the desert for us to shoot at were jeeps, trucks, trailers, armored cars and the occasional tank. The beautiful Sabre that we flew at Willy was equipped with what may or may not have been a state of the art gunsight. New or old, it seemed a marvelous device. Because it was designed to steer us to a place in the sky from which we could hit the target, or at least offer to steer us to that place. To properly respond to that offer, of course, we had to get the aircraft to do what the gunsight recommended. As I remember it, the gunsight presented itself to the pilot as a circle of orange spots, with a larger spot in the center. That circle appeared in the pilot's line of sight. It was a lighted pattern shining on the Plexiglas bubble canopy of the bird. If you flew the aircraft so as to put the pattern on your quarry, what you actually would be doing is putting the bird in a position so that bullets fired at that moment from its 50-caliber machine guns would zoom out to a point in front of the enemy aircraft where it would duly fly into them.

When we were getting organized for our first flight to go shoot at jeeps and trucks, we asked Fox how to use the gunsight on those targets. In his dry voice, he said, "You don't." We then asked what sighting method was used. He answered, "You'll be down on the deck. Just point your aircraft in the general direction of the target and start firing. You will see your slugs hitting the ground. Then walk 'em into the target. We'll be using the gunsight later on, when we do air-to-air."

So there we were, down on the deck again, out in the desert. No horses this time. Just, oops, right there, a truck convoy. We got here in combat formation, which provided space among aircraft. No longer were we tucked up, very close to each other, in echelon. Some days earlier, Fox had shown us this new formation arrangement. Its advantages were obvious. With ample spacing between birds, we were freed from concentrating continuously on maintaining tight, wing position and able instead to look around and, as necessary, maneuver independently while at the same time remaining in support of each other. Having spotted the trucks, I clicked my radio to tell the others and opened fire with the 50-caliber. As advertised, there out in front of me on the ground was a little parade of puffs made by slugs, a few yards to the right of the truck I hoped to hit. I bent the nose a little to the left and kept firing. The puffs also moved left then disappeared into the truck. Hits. Pieces of metal flew off. Kept firing, nose coming down as the bird got closer. Quit lest I fly into the truck. As usual, up and away.

The second time we were out shooting at trucks I experienced my one Willy emergency. Again I was down on the deck, perhaps twenty-five feet off the ground, firing, watching the conga line of puffs out front, moving the nose of the bird to adjust them up into what looked like a dump truck (why a dump truck ?). When Express Flight had discussed emergencies at our table some days before, Fox had mentioned a problem that occurred occasionally in the air conditioning system of the 86. Because at higher altitudes the air outside the aircraft is cold, air conditioning usually isn't needed in the bird. Heating is required. But, when flying is being done down close to the ground, where the outside air may be hot, air conditioning may be necessary. North American had given the F-86 an AC system. The problem Fox described occurs when the system malfunctions in some way, switching without warning from blowing cold air to blowing snow flakes. If the flake production is heavy, the canopy of the bird gets obscured and the pilot's visibility is adversely affected. If flake production is especially heavy, the pilot may find that he cannot see out of the cockpit at all.

That is what happened to me. Happily, the first part of the applicable emergency procedure came immediately to mind. Stop shooting. Switch to instrument flight. Because there weren't any mountains or big hills or tall buildings where we were shooting that morning, being unable to see out of the cockpit didn't put me in any particular danger. This was the case so long as the moment I took my finger off the trigger I also switched over to flying the gauges and didn't let the nose of the bird eat up the twenty-five feet of altitude we had enjoyed when the snow started. If there was danger, it wasn't to me but, instead, to the other three Express birds. Not being able to see, I might fly into them. So another early step in the applicable emergency procedure was to tell Fox, Dittrick and Cooledge what was going on in my bird. Just as Cooledge had used the radio to tell us of his speed brake problem, so I was permitted to use it to tell Express that my AC was making snow, that I couldn't see them or anything else outside the cockpit and that I was flying IFR, climbing out straight ahead. Fox immediately answered, "Understand. We'll stay out of your way." Then I took another emergency procedure step: I turned off the air conditioner! In a matter of seconds, the snow stopped and soon thereafter the canopy cleared, the big moment had passed and Express went back to machine gunning. It got warm in my cockpit but not too hot. Snowflakes would have been worse.

****

One morning a pair of visiting firemen appeared at the Express table. As I have already mentioned, we had had visits from singles. This was our first pair. They were captains. Older. Maybe in their early thirtiess, like the Germans. They behaved a little bit like check pilots, although they seemed somewhat tentative. Possibly they were check pilot candidates. One of them said he would fly flight lead. Dittrick would fly his wing. Fox and

Cooledge must have been elsewhere. The other captain said he would fly my wing, which meant that I would fly second element lead.

I do not remember what we did once we got to altitude. But I do remember the first part of the flight, which involved my getting the second element properly off the ground and then joined up with on the other captain and Dittrick. A challenge for second element lead, in making that first join up, as flight lead makes his gradual, climbing turn, waiting for you to come on, is to minimize the number of aileron movements and throttle adjustments on the way up. Because the perfect join-up would involve none of the former and just one of the latter. In other words, once you, as second element lead, set the bank angle and throttle position that you believe would bring you unalterably onto the wing of flight lead, you will change nothing—nothing—until you are able to take off just a smidge of power having arrived in ideal wing position, joining on flight lead. If you were able to do that, the trip upward for your wing man would have been smooth as silk and easy as pie. I had not yet managed it, either at Laughlin or at Willy. I had come close, having needed, on a couple of occasions, only a few aileron wiggles while sliding up the golden path. But I had never been perfect. This morning I was perfect. I changed nothing on the way up.

When the flight was over and the four of us were back at the table, flight lead began what sounded like checkride talk. Almost the first words, USAF officious words, out of his mouth were, "Three, the join-up was a bit on the ragged side." To my astonishment, the other captain, the one who had been on my wing, interrupted. He said, to my delight, "Whoa, Hoss. That was the best join-up I have ever seen." Perhaps he had date of rank on the other captain so it was easy for him to contradict him and praise me. Or perhaps he was junior and was willing to disagree with the other fellow anyway. Either way, it sounded like he meant it. So I was puffed. And gratified. I nudged Dittrick under the table.

The next day Express Flight was back together. If there were visiting firemen in the flight shack, they were calling on other people and not bothering us. Our discussion at table was intense. Because we would be doing air-to-air that morning. For the first time. I think we only did it three times during our stay at Willy. For me, it would be the peak of the Willy experience.

As previously described in this memoir, air-to-air practice at Willy in 1957 involved flights of four F-86Fs, each consisting of one instructor pilot and three rated pilots, making firing passes in a choreographed manner at a rectangular, canvas, target sleeve towed on a cable behind a T-33. The T-33 would fly a rectangular pattern. I believe the F-86Fs, each equipped with a single, 50-caliber machine gun, could fire at the sleeve only on the first long leg and the connected, second, short leg of the rectangle. The length of the two legs was fixed. This meant that, in order to maximize the number of firing passes, and thus enhance the likelihood of hits on the target, a four ship would need to arrive exactly on time at the first perch position, so it could get started at firing passes promptly, and then, as a foursome and as individuals, make each firing pass as precisely, and thus as efficiently, as possible. This efficiency would allow as many firing passes as possible to be made. Thus the challenge of the game was both in the flying and in the shooting.

The term "perch" refers to the location in the air alongside and above the target sleeve where each four ship would initially position itself before starting each firing pass. As I remember it, the perch was two, or perhaps three, 86 wing widths displaced from the flight path of the T-33 and the towed target and on the same heading.

The choreography went like this: flight lead would roll in toward the target, dive down toward it and start firing—and, unlike some Koreans, quit firing well before turning to pass behind the target. Then lead would overtake the target and the T-33 on the far side and fly parallel to them, leaving them behind. As soon as lead started firing, two would roll in. By the time two started firing, lead would be well beyond the T-33 on the far side and three would roll in. Then lead would be climbing back up toward the perch and, as he did that, four would roll in. At that moment, two would be beyond the T-33 on the far side and three would be firing. Then four would be firing with lead rolling in again and around all four of us would go.

As we tried our best to aim at the target, we were using, or at least trying to properly use, the orange circle of dots of the gunsight. However, I have no clear recollection of doing that. In the firing sequence we were following, the moments we had to put the circle on the sleeve were necessarily rushed and unavoidably brief. So the image of the sleeve behind the circle came and went very fast. It eventually occurred to us that the rush may be what we would experience in combat and thus what Willy wanted us to see and get accustomed to. Other things we encountered included the smell of gunpowder and the great exhilaration of the air-to-air flying itself. Down, fire, up and around, down, fire, up and around. Beautiful Sabres, were we eagles? Were we angels?

I wish I could compare our performance with the air-to-air work of other Willy flights of the day. Undoubtedly there were some which thought of themselves as hotshots, as we of Express Flight thought of ourselves. Unfortunately, the only flight I had seen shooting at the sleeve close up was the four ship which included the Koreans. Their performance would hardly qualify as a standard against which to measure ours. Where they were ragged and hesitant, I thought we were precise and decisive. Where their coordination was marginal, ours was exact. As I watched the maneuvers of Fox, Dittrick and Cooledge, and as I flew my own beautiful Sabre, our individual flying seemed flawless. As the air-to-air pattern of Express Flight unfolded, with the four of us attacking the target in turn, making firing pass after firing pass with our spacing and timing just right, we seemed to be performing in close to perfect, if not perfect, harmony. Surely air-to-air was, for us, another Air Force gift.

When the T-33 towing the target turned left onto the second leg of the rectangle, we, the shooting foursome, magically relocated our perch to the new direction and immediately resumed our exact roundelay. Something unexpected on that first air-to-air day then happened, far out to our left. Three 86s were together, heading away, with a fourth joining up. As he, with his nose up, approached second element lead, number four rolled his aircraft. We saw all this in glimpses as we continued firing. Later we learned that the three birds, with four joining, had also been doing air-to-air—we never knew exactly where—and that the boy who had done the roll on his way up had been chastised. By way of explanation, he had said, "All I was doing was a victory roll, sir." The three of us knew just how he felt.

Back on the ground, we were told where we could go to look at the target sleeve we had been shooting at. The 50-caliber machine gun bullets in each of our birds were painted with a different color. If hits have been made on the sleeve, each hole torn in the canvas would bear the color of the shooter. When we inspected the sleeve that day, there were no holes in it. A few days later, we had another session of air-to-air. The flying was as thrilling as it was the first time. The shooting also must have been the same. Because again, no hits were achieved. On our third and final try, we flew, we thought, with special skill. We fired away with great hope. When we inspected the target sleeve that midday, all of us eagerly looking, there were a half a dozen holes to be seen. Each was rimmed in red. The bullets in my beautiful Sabre had been painted red. Those were my hits.

Not many months later, my Air Force days came to an end. After Willy, I had asked to go to Korea, guided by Lieutenant Fox's enthusiastic and somewhat bloodthirsty reminder that it was still possible to shoot at people there. But the USAF no longer sent married pilots to the Far East. That was now seen as too expensive.

So, with Dittrick from Express Flight, I was assigned to the 524th Fighter Bomber Squadron at Bergstrom AFB in Austin, Texas. The 524th had flown combat in Korea, carrying out air to ground missions in the straight wing F 84. Jimmy Doolittle's son John, a major, was the commanding officer. In World War II, John had flown combat missions in the B-26 from bases in England and then the European continent. I thought he might have received his B-26 training at Laughlin AFB. I planned to ask him about that when I met him. But I didn't get the chance. The day after I signed in at the 524th, Major Doolittle was found dead beneath his desk, having shot himself in the head with his Colt 45 pistol. Perhaps being the son of one of the most famous of military men was too great a burden.

Until recently, the 524th at Bergstrom flew the swept wing F-84F, the bird that had the bad reputation at Luke AFB and elsewhere. The squadron, to the relief of its pilots, had been notified that its complement of F 84Fs was to be retired. The replacement aircraft would be the McDonnell F 101, called the Voodoo. The process of supplanting F 84Fs with 101s had already begun.

A big, twin-engine, supersonic aircraft, the 101 was a fast, high performance bird. It would soon set a transcontinental speed record. The pilots of the 524th, while happy to get away from the F 84F and move into a hot aircraft, were at the same time leery of the 101. It was considered somewhat unforgiving. It had a disconcerting tendency to abruptly pitch up in certain airspeed and attitude situations. The 524th consensus was that a conservative approach to the 101 was therefore indicated. Transition from the F 84F to the Voodoo was proceeding cautiously. Dittrick and I noticed that 101s returning to Bergstrom weren't using the overhead approach. No one pitched out in a 101. The landing pattern that the 101 jocks used was the big rectangle we had last seen at primary flight school. Surreptitiously, Dittrick and I called it a bomber pattern, somewhat scornfully. We did not use the term bomber pattern where 524th pilots could hear us.

Both of us wanted to fly the 101. We were Willy boys, after all. We were not put off by the conservative attitudes of the 524th. But, quite unexpectedly, the Air Force threw up a roadblock. It told us that we could not fly the F 101, or any other fighter aircraft, for that matter, unless we were willing to extend our tours of active duty. I believe we were required to sign up for an additional three years. In 1955, when I was commissioned, I had originally committed for three years. Now, in order to continue flying, I would be obliged to serve for a total of six years. It seemed to me this would make sense only if I were willing to commit to an Air Force career.

In the months just before reporting for active duty, I had worked for Exxon. I had liked it and had tentatively decided to return to a career in the oil industry, once my three year Air Force commitment was complete. Now I had to fish or cut bait. If I had been permitted to take on the F 101 and then leave the Air Force at the end of my original commitment of three years, I would have gladly done that. Even if the cost of continuing to fly fighters was extending for an additional year, thus serving until the end of a fourth year, I would have done that. I enjoyed flying. I thought of myself as a fighter pilot, even if wet behind the ears. But staying until the end of six years seemed too much. My oil industry life would be too long deferred. So I decided to leave the Air Force and so advised the officers in charge at Bergstrom. In a matter of months, I was sent home, honorably discharged.

My father had asked that I serve as a military officer. He believed that was the proper way for me to discharge the obligation to the country that attached to our life of privilege. What I understood him to mean, in a general sense, was that I should make a gift to America—in return for privilege given me. I should give my service, preferably in the leadership role that came with the status of officer. I had gladly agreed to do that.

Now my service was done and, indeed, gifts had been given. Had giving been done by me? I suppose yes, but only in the most minor of ways. I felt the real gifts were ones that were given *to* me. The United States Air Force had taken me in and taught me things that must be learned by men who fly fighter planes— fighter aircraft—in order to fight for and defend the country. To me, those were precious things. They far, far outweighed what I had contributed. I was thankful for them.

Epilogue

OUR FATHERS WERE PATRIOTIC MEN. They had gone to war willingly. They had served their country well. In at least one way, they were a special breed of patriot. Their fathers, and their fathers' fathers, had prospered greatly in America. Thus the men who bore us, and raised us, were men of privilege. So there was in their patriotism a vibrant element of indebtedness. Because they had been given American lives of ease and comfort, and because they knew full well that their lives were different from —in many ways better than—those of most of their fellow citizens, when the country was threatened their instinct to defend her was based in good measure on the idea that they owed her.

They lived that idea and passed it on to their sons. I was one of those sons. Like my father and his father before him, I bore an Ivy League mark. It bespoke privilege. We studied at Princeton University. Even if nothing else identified me as a privileged boy, my wearing the Princeton label did.

My father's willingness to send me to Princeton had depended on my promising him that I would serve in the military of the United States, preferably as an officer, when I graduated. I agreed to do that, discovering when I arrived at Princeton that hundreds of my classmates had made the same commitment. Little did we know that we were among the last of a dwindling tribe. In the

decades that followed our time at Princeton, military Reserve
Officer Training Units shriveled at Ivy League schools and
disappeared altogether at many American colleges. The military
draft was discontinued. Military service, at both the enlisted and
the officer level, became an occupation of the few: working poor,
minorities and the otherwise disenfranchised, rarely taken up any
more by boys, or girls, of privilege.

My son is a privileged American, as is his son. My Princeton
classmates' sons, and their sons, are privileged also. None has
served in the military of the United States. I did not demand it of
my son nor did he of his. At this late moment in life I find myself
somewhat puzzled that neither of us did. I enjoyed my short tour
in the Air Force. I loved the F 86F, the beautiful Sabre. My
Princeton friends who flew fighters were equally fond of the
experience. But none of their sons or grandsons has served.
Perhaps the fathers did not even suggest it.

Why not? I cannot speak for them. But surely the most
important reason neither I nor my son urged our sons to serve
was the absence of the kind of war that affected my father. Not
that there weren't conflicts in the world around us. In my lifetime
and in my son's, there was the Vietnam War, the Middle East
Wars and the Afghanistan War. But in none of those struggles
was the United States itself threatened. As a result, in the most
profound sense, the country's heart was not engaged. In turn, the
military services have become disconnected from the citizenry
at large, necessarily going in one direction while the populace as
a whole was going in another. They have all too frequently been
dying while wondering who cares. Spit upon in the Vietnam War,
ignored in the Iraq and Afghanistan Wars.

I came to know some military men who would in later years
occupy that bitter predicament in the course of my brief stay in
the 524th Fighter Bomber Squadron in 1958 in Austin. At a

distance, the Vietnam War was already beginning to appear. Dittrick and I, new boys from Willy, were made welcome as temporary members of the Squadron. The Air Force powers that be had not yet decided what to do with us.

I remember three members of the 524th in particular. One was Lieutenant Terry Graese. I had known him slightly at Laughlin AFB, where he had been an instructor while I was there. He was my age and looked even younger. When Dittrick and I caught up with him in the 524th, he had already checked out in the F 101. It was he who told us about the bird's propensity to pitch up. I believe he said, sensibly enough, that the problem was particularly troublesome if it happened on final approach, when the aircraft was low and slow. In that situation, an unexpected, exaggerated nose up stall would be especially unwelcome.

Another 524th fellow who talked with me was a grizzled, older man, a captain, who quite suddenly one morning as we were sitting around in the 524th's flight shack asked me what I thought he should do if his 101 suffered a flameout on takeoff. I was taken aback. Did this veteran fellow, who had flown air-to-ground combat in Korea and who, for all I knew, had even fought in World War II, at the tail end, really want my opinion? Or was he just testing me? Or both!

When I looked at him blankly at first, he answered his own question, saying, "I suppose you'd recommend putting the nose smack down and landing straight ahead, right?" I belatedly nodded, realizing in dismay that, in all the months I had been flying, I had never given serious thought to what I would do if I were to lose an engine on takeoff. I had a queasy feeling. How heedless was I? Did I really think that the problem would never come up? Although I knew I should chase after the captain and thank him for making me think, I feared I would look like a school boy. So, shamefacedly, I let the moment pass.

The third 524th pilot that we came to know was Captain Robbie Robinson. He was only slightly older than we were. He also had flown air to ground missions in Korea in the straight wing F 84. His aircraft had been hit by ground fire on more than one occasion. Twice he had been wounded in the feet and lower legs. As a result, he walked with a slight but noticeable limp. Like Terry Graese and the flameout-on-takeoff captain, Robbie hoped to make the Air Force a career. Unlike Dittrick and me, neither Robbie nor the other two officers had graduated college. They had either gone directly from high school to fight in the Korean War and had earned their commissions in OCS or had left college before graduation and earned their commissions as aviation cadets. Their hope now was that their war service would stand them in good stead, offsetting their lack of a degree.

Robbie and his wife Jo became friends of my wife and me in Austin. On my return to civilian life in New Jersey, I discovered, somewhat to my surprise, that there was available to me ongoing contact with him. Contact with Robbie was through his uncle, Francis Robinson, who was press, television and tour director for the Metropolitan Opera in New York City. At the time, my mother, who lived in the city, had box seat season tickets at the Met. As her guests, my wife and I regularly attended performances. Alerted by Robbie to his and Jo's acquaintance with my wife and me, Francis Robinson from time to time invited the three of us to have lunch with him at the opera house. He was a charming, gracious, sophisticated man who thought of Robbie as a son. He kept us informed of Robbie's Air Force assignments and, in the early 1960s, was proud to report that Robbie has been promoted major.

A year or two later, with the Vietnam War in full swing, he told us that Robbie had received orders to Vietnam. He was by then flying one of the big fighter planes of the day, either the F-4 McDonnell Douglas Phantom or the F-105 Republic Thunderchief.

Then one day, Francis Robinson telephoned to tell us that Robbie had died. Preparing to go overseas, he had had a mid-air collision over the Gulf of Mexico. Francis Robinson was devastated. Was Robbie killed in the collision? Or did he drown in the Gulf? We never knew. His body wasn't recovered.

A couple of years later, in 1969, with the Vietnam War continuing, I wrote to Paul Nitze, Deputy Secretary of Defense, volunteering to rejoin the Air Force in order to fly fighter aircraft in Vietnam. Paul Nitze was married to my brother's wife's aunt and we had met briefly at family functions. In due course, Secretary Nitze responded. He stated that the F-86 F, the military aircraft I had most recently flown, was no longer carried in the inventory of the Air Force, adding that my training as a fighter pilot in the mid 1950s was out of date. Explaining that it would be expensive to train me to fly the fighter aircraft currently in service, he stated that, if I nonetheless was determined to rejoin the Air Force, I would be welcome to take a non-flying, administrative job. He added that he would be happy to steer me toward such an assignment.

I wrote Mr. Nitze back, thanked him for his response and told him I was not interested in a non-flying job.

About the Author

EDWARD K. MILLS II WAS BORN IN New York City in 1934. He graduated Princeton University in 1955 with honors in The Special Program in the Humanities and English. He served in the United States Air Force from 1956 through 1958. He was trained as a single-engine jet fighter pilot. He then worked for nineteen years for Exxon Corporation, serving in various capacities including Manager of Public Affairs for the United States. He later served as Chief Executive Officer of North Atlantic Refining Ltd. in Newfoundland, Canada. In addition, he owned and operated contracting companies providing technical and logistical services to the oil industry in the United States and overseas. Mr. Mills is married, has three grown children and lives in Florida.